My Soul Contract

A Teaching Memoir of
Trauma, Truth, and Transformation

Micki Abels

DEDICATION

To All My Teachers
Past, Present, & Future

To my three favorite guys in the whole world
Russell, my rock, my consistently supportive and patient husband
Nicholas and Derrick, my adoring and admirable sons.
I am honored to be your wife and mother.

Thank you for choosing me.

Table of Contents

MY SOUL CONTRACT

Preface

I wasn't always like this. I was content to follow along for the sake of fitting in. A well-trained chameleon, I learned how to be whom or what others needed me to be. I was not accustomed to questioning my needs, as long as I was confident believing the people around me were happy. But then my predictable world turned upside down, forcing me into a world of the unknown.

I continue to be surprised by my experiences, inviting brilliant, unpredictable answers to my questions. I have acquired an inexplicable thirst for knowledge, like nothing I have ever yearned for in my lifetime thus far. I welcome the unknown. In fact, I am in awe of it. Somehow the unknown feels like the embrace of a familiar friend, and I have fallen in love with the encouraging sense of freedom it offers. The desire to question my beliefs has confirmed my purpose in this life and has offered a heightened confidence to accept my truth. The lessons have been a gradual introduction to my authentic spirit. I have recognized and secured an inner knowing, that, to the best of my ability to explain, was born in me and within it lies an unshakable responsibility to remain connected to its voice.

My teaching memoir is my life's journey of personal transformation, self-discovery, and evolution. I share my experiences of inviting the unknown while allowing signs and symbols to guide my soul to a world beyond the physical. I share the wisdom my spiritual teachers provided as I developed a healthy trust to explore the life that was patiently waiting for me. I share the tools and processes I've adopted to nurture my spirit while introducing an honest internal dialogue.

Along the way, I had so many questions and I felt a magnetic pull towards my purpose.

My intention is to be of service by sharing my experiences with those who are attempting to navigate life's uncertainty. I am healing, we are all healing at different warps on different journeys. These are my stories told from my point of view. They are based on my recollections, my perspective, and my opinions.

This is the testimony of my soul's journey, my exploration, and my destiny. Herein are my stories of trauma and transformation and how my experiences led me to discover my soul's truth—my soul contract.

Embrace the beautiful, simple, and pure abundance this life has in store for you. Ask and be open to receive. It is all waiting for you.

MY SOUL CONTRACT

Part I-Breathe

Caterpillar

In the first seven years of human life we are like sponges, absorbing our environment through simple observation. Because our brains can only establish analytical thinking through our observations, we adopt and mimic the behaviors we observe. As life continues, we develop stories based on these foundational observations. They become deeply ingrained into our subconscious and become part of our personality. Our personalities are formed based on the memories of our experiences. We operate unconsciously from these learned behaviors, and our behaviors become our programs. We seldom question the programs when our lives are running smoothly; however, oftentimes it is when a traumatic or shocking event occurs that we begin to question all of our programs.

All humans have a consciousness and an ego. Most of us have experienced some form of trauma, pain, or loss in our lives. It is within our ego's nature to habitually increase the dose of negativity surrounding our stories of pain to perpetually offer those feelings a front row seat while continually breathing life into them, making our stories our personal reality. Our stories become our identity, and without our attachment to the stories, we lose our identity and feel lost. We remain in the pain of our stories because it is familiar, and within the familiar lives a certain feeling of connection and comfort.

My stories are not necessarily in chronological order, but in order of importance to my healing process. Through deep introspection, I realized that I used the emotions of pain and betrayal to fuel my resentment that kept me tethered to my past. I learned how to pay attention to my heart, listen to my spirit, and let go of old beliefs to reveal my authenticity.

Chapter 1

The Path That Leads Back

Oftentimes it is one incredibly difficult event that breaks our hearts into a space that craves the introduction of our spiritual growth. The soul is waiting with anticipation as the spirit acknowledges the true path to fulfill and feed the heart with inner peace. I believe that everything happens for us, to lead us back to whole.

I stand on the sidelines, waiting to be noticed, hoping nobody does. Yearning for, but not wanting the attention. I am spotlessly clean. I have dirty elbows and snarly hair. I am smart and a smart-ass. I am pretty plain. I am kind and sweet if you are kind and sweet to me. I love my family and friends conditionally and my pets unconditionally. I am patiently impatient. I am jumping up and down standing perfectly still, screaming silently, *Pick me, pick me. Don't pick me.* I am funny and use humor to make my point. I am serious, outgoing, and shy. I dream of being spontaneous as long as it doesn't disrupt my schedule. I am on the fence most of the time, somewhere in between trying to decide which life is mine. I am small. I am invisible.

Do I matter? Why am I here?

I speak my truth without desire to please. I surround myself with like-minded individuals. I am no stranger to struggles, betrayal, and pain. I am no stranger to pure joy, inner peace, and constant gratitude. I acknowledged my true path and discovered which beliefs are mine. I pay attention to my heart and endure to ignore my ego most of the time. This practice takes constant effort and attention, and I have no regrets as my experiences have tugged at my heart and steered its direction. I have the loving support of my family and dear friends who have stood alongside me while I was introduced to the life that was patiently waiting for me. I am energy. I am light. I am love.

I matter and I know why I am here.

Most days I know why I am here. But there are many days I am the skinned-knee child crying out for answers, trying to understand the pain within the truths the lessons offer.

My healing journey began in 2005, but the trouble with my parents had been brewing long before that. It was 2005 when I decided to have a difficult conversation with them. That conversation would lead to the end of our relationship as I knew it.

Over the years, I had conditioned myself into making excuses for my parents' behavior. I made excuses for the years of blatant favoritism toward my younger sister and her family. Excuses for years of my parents taking advantage of my husband's generous nature, and excuses for the years of making my boys feel left out. I had conditioned myself to believe they never meant any of it. I allowed my excuses to protect me, my husband, and my sons.

I had reached my breaking point, and the excuses that got my parents off the hook for years had come to an end. I was angry and hurt, betrayed and pissed off.

I am the middle child in a family of three daughters. I personify the definition of the middle child syndrome, caught in between my two sisters, never the favorite. From external observances, my parents were perfect. They appeared to live a carefree life. They both had a great sense of humor and they loved to laugh. They did a spectacular job of ensuring that our family seemed to be perfect in every way. My parents had a perfect marriage and raised three perfect daughters. My parents could boast that their three perfect daughters, (the three queens, as we had been nicknamed) had three perfect marriages of their own. My parents had perfect grandchildren and a perfect home in a perfect town. For a long time, I thought I was perfect. *How could I not be perfect with all that perfection around me?* My biggest fear in life was that I would disappoint my parents. That fear became a reality when I had to share a not-so-perfect truth with them.

MY SOUL CONTRACT

Chapter 2

Our Love Story

My husband, Russ, and I were high school sweethearts. We began dating in summer of 1979, between our sophomore and junior year. We were sixteen years old and we fell in love.

To me, Russ is a teddy bear with a big heart. He is as strong as he is gentle. He stands 6'1" with broad shoulders, big muscles, and a smile that makes me feel like I am the only person in the room. He is confident and direct. He speaks his mind with diplomacy. He is smart and pays attention to detail. I knew he wouldn't take any shit from anyone, and he doesn't have any trouble letting you know when you cross the line with him. He is kind and honorable and treats me with respect. He smells good and he feels good and he is so handsome. When I was sixteen, I felt safe and protected in his presence and I wanted nothing more than to spend every minute of every day with him. Still do.

Neither one of us attended college. I had worked for my parents in our family business but wanted to leave and join the banking industry—more specifically, I wanted to be a bank teller. In

1981, the year I graduated high school, I applied and was offered a full-time teller position at our hometown bank.

Russ had always been interested in cars and wanted to follow his passion of becoming an auto mechanic. He loved fixing cars and is very good at it. He began working for a local dealership when he was sixteen, and that is where he works to this day.

We worked and saved our money, and Russ proposed to me on my golden birthday in January of 1985. We were married in October 1986 and were blessed with the birth of our first son, Nicholas, in 1990. Fourteen months after Nicholas was born, we were blessed with our second son, Derrick. In April 1992, we moved out of our small two-bedroom condominium in south suburban Illinois to a ranch-style home on two acres in a small rural town just thirty miles south of where we grew up. We raised our sons in our cozy, country home and it is where we plan to live until our retirement.

Chapter 3

The Store

In 2002, Russ and I opened a small business with my sister and her husband. We decided to operate the grocery store that had been in our small country town for years. When we moved here in 1992, Dan and Shirley owned and operated the store and seemed to have done well for themselves. They were genuine and kind and made it a point to get to know my family and call us by name. Our town and all of the people in it felt as if we had gone back in time, and I adored the close-knit feeling our newly adopted town offered my young family. I referred to it as my *little Mayberry*. We could buy anything we needed at our little store, including fresh-cut meat, a nice assortment of produce, and dry goods. We could even rent a movie if we wanted.

When Dan and Shirley decided to sell, another family bought the store and put their own ideas into it. They kept some of the same things Dan and Shirley had and changed others. When the second owners sold it to us we allowed ourselves thirty days to give it a fresh, clean look. We worked eighteen-hour days getting the store ready to open. The kids would come after school, and when their homework was complete, they would help in whatever way they could. We scrubbed it from top to bottom, rearranged some shelving, and gave it a fresh coat of paint.

Our vision was to offer our customers a fresh daily selection of everything they would find at a larger supermarket but on a smaller scale. We wanted to bring back what we had experienced when we first moved here and restore that country charm we had grown to adore.

My sister and her husband had years of experience running their own business. Russ and I certainly had enough ambition and interest to learn everything we needed to in order to run a successful grocery store. We worked together on a business plan, hired employees, and prepared the store for opening day. We hired Dan, the original owner, as our butcher, and he taught my brother-in-law (and eventually me) how to cut meat and display a mouth-watering presentation in the butcher case. We knew the townspeople would be happy to see a familiar face at the butcher counter, and we were so grateful for Dan's involvement.

As we prepared to open, my sister and brother-in-law told us that they were unable to come up with the funds needed to have equal ownership of the business. We had worked so hard to open the store within our thirty day time frame, so Russ and I agreed to extend the terms of our agreement. We trusted, as they told us, that they were doing everything within their power to honor our agreement.

We opened for business in October 2002. By December, we learned that our main supplier had filed bankruptcy and they could not fill our orders to capacity. While we searched for another supplier, our shelves were looking sparse. We asked our patrons to be patient while we dealt with the unexpected curveball.

I was the general manager, did the accounting for the business, and learned how to design our sales ads. I ordered everything in the store with the exception of meat and liquor. My brother-in-law took care of those two large expenses. The four of us decided, after I became more confident about what was needed on the higher-cost items, I would transition into ordering those as well.

The day-to-day business activities were my brother-in-law's and my responsibilities. Russ kept his job as an automobile technician so that we would continue to have health insurance, at least until the business could support those expenses. Russ came to the store after work each night and spent weekends meeting our customers, working behind the meat counter, and repairing a laundry list of failed equipment. My sister would come in a few hours a week to give me a break or allow me an opportunity to attend the boys' school or sporting events.

Our daily homemade hot meals were a success, and we began to take orders for catered events. At Thanksgiving we offered roast turkey with all the fixings, and that proved to be a big hit. We decided to offer turkey, prime rib, and ham dinners for Christmas, and we received a good response from our customers for those as well.

About a week before Christmas, a huge order from our meat supplier had been delivered, and I assumed our catering orders had increased. Because of the increase in orders, my brother-in-law showed me how to prep and cook the prime rib so that I could help in getting the meals ready for our customers. After all, he still had his own business to run.

The holidays had come and gone. Business was steady, the store was busy, and it was starting to feel good. But when I pulled the figures from the profit-and-loss sheet for December, I was shocked. The first two months of business were not profitable, but December should have been, but the numbers on the report proved the opposite.

Concerned, I asked a trusted friend who was a business and finance consultant to offer his advice. After scouring through our financial reports he suspected something strange was going on. He suggested that I keep a very close eye on all operations and gain a true understanding of the store's profit and loss at the close of business each day.

He also advised Russ and me to conduct a count of inventory every evening after close. It would determine which departments were losing money and how much. We followed his advice while I kept a close eye on all aspects of our operations. I was aware of what had been ordered and delivered, what was sold, and what was considered waste.

Our daily inventory counts proved that items such as liquor and meat were ordered but were no longer in inventory, yet we did not have the cash register receipts to support the sales of those goods.

It was now the fall of 2003 and we had extended our agreement with my sister and brother-in-law for months, but they were still unable to come up with their half of the money for the store. We asked them to meet with us. Russ and I told them about the discrepancies we found concerning sales versus inventory. We explained that our findings supported our suspicions and we were prepared to provide all of the documentation from our nightly inventory proving that something was very wrong. I expected a reaction of shock and confusion. I expected my sister and bother-in-law to deny any involvement of unethical behavior. I expected an argument about our findings. I expected them to ask us to present the documentation and to explain it. None of those things happened. They never denied involvement nor asked to see our documentation. They were not confused and they didn't argue. Their lack of reaction was strange.

Russ and I explained that we could no longer extend our agreement with them and told my sister and her husband that they had to withdraw their involvement and leave the business. It was a highly uncomfortable conversation to have with my family, and I hated that they had put me and Russ in that position. I cried and my sister cried.

That evening, before we parted ways, we all agreed that it was paramount that we kept our business and our family relationships separate. We did not want our kids and our families to be negatively affected by our business decision.

The next responsibility we had was to tell my parents about the business decisions that had been made. I volunteered to do that myself.

As I stood trembling and feeling as though I would vomit, I told my parents the details that led to the dissolution of what was intended to be an exciting business venture between their daughters and their families. My mother's response was to conveniently excuse my sister and brother-in-law's choices. My dad, on the other hand, offered his support. He placed his hand on my shoulder and looked into my tear-filled eyes and said, "Do what you have to do, Mic, it'll be all right."

Before leaving my parent's home that night, the four of us agreed, just as my sister and brother-in-law had agreed, we would not allow our business decisions to affect our family.

Our perfect family.

Russ and I made a genuine effort to keep our business and personal lives separate, but there was an undeniable strain between our families. Following our business separation, my family of four had been excluded from the usual family gatherings. When we were invited and attended an event, we were ignored. Tensions grew within my family and at the store.

After our main supplier of the store filed bankruptcy a few months back, we had to choose a new supplier. The new supplier charged twice as much for the same service as our original supplier. Between that and the increased cost of goods, we were spending more money than we were taking in. Russ and I decided to downsize the store, to use less square footage in an attempt to accommodate the changes we were facing. With less to offer, we could no longer compete with the larger supermarket prices, and over the next several months we lost the support of our community. We continued to bleed money and made the decision to close the store in August 2004.

During the last Saturday of our going-out-of-business sale, Nick and I were sitting alone at the store. I could tell he wanted to ask me something, but he was holding back. I assured him that he could ask me anything and feel safe doing so. After some gentle coaxing, armed with his fourteen-year-old courage, he asked, "Why do Gramma and Bup treat us differently than our cousins?"

My heart broke into a million pieces as I realized that all of my excuses for my parents' behavior had done nothing to protect their hearts. Gazing into my son's sad eyes, I could no longer make excuses for them.

All the emotions, all my memories of the inequities came flooding in. Growing up, I was treated differently than my younger sister, and my children were treated differently than my younger sister's children. *Why were my sons, who were well-behaved and courteous, being silenced with accusatory looks? Why were my children ignored or blamed for things they didn't do? Why did my parents exclude my sons from special events? Why did my children have to hide their jealousy and listen politely as their cousins shared the fun things they were invited to do with Gramma and Bup? Why didn't my sons have a grandma and grandpa cheering section at their baseball or basketball games? Why did I feel that when I brought my boys to visit my parents it was an intrusion rather than a joy?*

Years and years of feeling left out was a personal and private pain that I believed I had been suffering alone. Following our business decision, it was clear who my parents supported, and it wasn't me or my husband or our sons. I had shouldered my parents' lack of interest in my life for long enough, and I had done so all in the name of family. But this didn't feel like family, and their actions were affecting my boys.

Everyone has a tipping point, and that was mine.

When Nick confessed his hurt, something stirred in me that I could no longer ignore. I couldn't allow my parents' behavior to continue, and I knew I had to speak up. My instinct as a mother was to protect my sons and ensure their physical and emotional safety. I felt a conviction, a survivalist, protective nature that ignited my motive, knowing we all deserved better.

I put off speaking with my parents while Russ and I closed the store. Before we knew it, the holidays were upon us and we spent an uncomfortable and awkward Christmas with my side of the family. The day after Christmas, we celebrated Derrick's birthday and, as was customary, we invited Mom, Dad, my sister, brother-in-law, and their kids to help celebrate.

Russ's sister, Dawn, and our nephew, Alex, were visiting from California and stayed with us for the holidays. The boys and their cousins always enjoyed their time together, and we didn't want them missing out on the usual activities.

Mom and Dad arrived and took their usual spot on the love seat in the living room. I was standing at the corner of the living room with a clear view of our driveway when I saw my sister pull in. She got out, and I noticed the exhaust billowing out of her car's muffler in the cold winter air. *Why didn't she shut the car off?* I opened the back door to greet her and her crew in the kitchen. Her disposition was as cold as the frosty air as she helped her kids out of their winter coats. She handed all of their coats to the two oldest girls and pointed to my bedroom. As she instructed the girls to put the coats on my bed, she reminded her kids that Gramma and Bup would drive them home. She clenched the front of her coat around her body, making it clear she did not plan on staying. I asked, "Aren't you staying for D's birthday?"

Without making eye contact, she said, "No, I have to go."

She left without saying happy birthday to Derrick. She left without saying hi to Dawn and Alex, and turned around and left my house. Clearly, my parents knew of her plan, and when I asked them what was going on, they shrugged their shoulders in obvious denial.

I hate confrontation. The holidays were over, and I knew it was time to face the strain I had been feeling with my parents head on.

To simplify my process, I prepared a written dialogue, a letter of sorts that I began to rehearse. With practice, I was surprised at how well I was able to keep my composure and relay my thoughts. I knew I had an enormous task ahead of me because it had not been my experience to witness my parents resolve conflict. Their typical reaction to problems was to ignore them or avoid any uncomfortable topics until the problem faded away.

I had expectations for a different outcome.

It occurred to me one afternoon while rehearsing my dialogue that there were toxic behavioral patterns on my mother's side of the family. It became clear to me that we, my mother and I, were repeating a similar pattern.

My intention was to discuss the topics that resulted in my distressed relationship with my parents, to explain how hurt I was, knowing that they chose to support my sister and brother-in-law over Russ and me. My intention was to explain how hurt I was that my boys were being treated as if they had done something wrong, and to have an adult conversation and to be heard.

Chapter 4

The Confrontation

About a month after Derrick's birthday, I arrived unannounced at my parents' home on a Saturday morning in the winter of 2005. It was important to me that they both be present, and a Saturday morning practically guaranteed that I would catch them both at the house.

When I arrived, my mom told me that my dad had made other plans for the day. Although it would have been easy for me to leave at that point, (after all, I had rehearsed my script with both parents accounted for) I mustered up the courage to stay. With my kids' best interest at heart, I said everything I intended to say. I shared my epiphany about the toxic patterns on my mom's side of the family. I reminded my mother of the conflict she experienced with her mother years earlier that resulted in their discord and eventual separation. I offered that there was a resemblance between what she and I were going through and what she went through with her mother. I reminded my mom that she had felt the same way I did. My mother had resentment toward her parents for the exact same reasons I resented my parents. I said, "Mom, the only difference between what happened between you and your mom and what is happening between you and me is that in our situation, I am you."

My eyes filled with tears as I spoke. My tears held my sons' hurt and my personal feelings of betrayal. My tears held the pain of hurting my mother as the truth poured off my tongue.

Feeling as though I had introduced the answer to our problems by comparing our similar experiences, I waited with anticipation for her acknowledgment. At that moment, I was able to breathe like I hadn't in months. A full breath in, filling my lungs to capacity. I felt my heart fill with hope. Hope that we could be fixed. Hope that our relationship could be fixed.

Confused, she looked at me with her forked brow and wrinkled forehead and shook her head from side to side, denying any similarities between our situations *at all*. Her negative response punctured my heart, and all hope drifted out with my exhausted breath.

As our conversation continued, it became crystal clear that the waters of understanding had been muddied. The familial threads that connected us were frayed. I listened to my mother tangle the truth and dismember my hope. I found it difficult to comprehend her reactions. She made several attempts to lighten the mood and change the subject. She darted from one topic to another. She made jokes and laughed and then asked me, with tears in her eyes, "What's going to happen when I die?"

I rehearsed what I needed to say because I anticipated her antics. By rehearsing, I was able to keep the conversation on track. I was able to complete my thoughts as I navigated through her attempts to make me break into an emotional mess. I offered my mom an opportunity to understand her own family history and recognize old wounds. At that point in my life, I realized I had played the role of who my mother needed me to be for far too long. I offered a grown-up conversation with a resolution, and she ignored it. She went so far as to laugh at it. I was open and vulnerable because that was all I had left. I was honest, and before I left I told my mother a well-rehearsed thought. "Mom, at the age of forty-two, I no longer need your approval and support, but it would be nice to know that I have it."

That well-rehearsed thought was my line in the sand. I left her house knowing I had fought for all of us and especially for Nicholas and Derrick. I felt strong. I felt courageous. I was proud of myself. I was emotionally exhausted.

I hated that my truth hurt my mom. I hated the daughter I had to be.

I left knowing I had given her a lot to sort through and think about. I knew she was hurt and I felt bad about that but hoped that at the very least we would agree to disagree. I expected that she would share our conversation with my dad and she would follow up with a phone call the next day.

My mom didn't call the next day. I figured my folks needed more time to sort through their feelings, so I waited a couple more days. With no response after a few days, I waited another week. And then I waited two weeks. One month. Two months. Six months. One year. Two years. Two and a half years.

During those two and a half years, my parents and I didn't speak. I spent a good portion of that time feeling like the kid that disappointed her parents, hiding in my teenage bedroom, waiting and wanting my mom and dad to come in and tell me everything would be okay. But this time was different. This time they retracted so far and for so long, it was obvious they wanted nothing to do with me. They did not come back. They weren't ever going to come back. They hurt me and I hurt them. The emotional betrayal of that acknowledgment was enormous, and it turned even the good parts of what I believed our relationship to be into a sour, messed-up reality.

Thirty months was enough time to mourn the emotional loss of my parents. I realized how different an emotional loss was than a physical loss. They were still living and breathing but chose to have nothing to do with me or their son-in-law or their grandsons. In many ways, it was more difficult than if they had died.

I spent those months in deep sadness about so many things. I was sad that we couldn't open our mouths to say what we should have said. I felt pain, betrayal, hurt, shame, guilt, loss, lack, hope, want, neglect and abandonment at a very deep emotional level.

I felt everything. I wanted to feel nothing. I wanted to kiss and make up. I wanted to stay mad forever. This wasn't supposed to happen. I was blind. I was naïve. I was stupid.

I. Was.

And now I Am.

I became nothing I wanted to be. I was not me. I was the most lost I had ever been. My direction was anywhere but here.

Chapter 5

Ditches, Bleachers, and BS

The slow-motion rotation spins my head into a dreamlike state. A blinding white wall of snow pulls me toward my statuesque position. I am perfectly situated to simply watch. Watch with my heart as it yearns for a different outcome. A moment that begs for observation.

Don't speak. Don't cry. Don't react.

Don't. Won't. Can't.

I had driven the same route to work Monday through Friday for years. On this particular winter morning, with the snow covering a precise patch of road, I was reminded of a troublesome incident that had occurred in 2007 and tossed our truck and my heart into the ditch.

It was about 7:15 a.m. when I had left for work. I was traveling cautiously over a blanket of fresh snow that had fallen over the ice-covered roads the night before. As I reached the top of a slight incline, less than a half mile on the opposite of the road, I saw one of my son's classmates traveling toward me. At that moment, without notice, I hit a patch of ice, and the tail end of my pickup truck spun to the right and then to the left. I attempted to steer the truck but lost control as the tires sprayed fresh snow all around the windows, blocking my view of the road. I couldn't tell where I was or in which direction I was headed. I prayed that I would not hit the kid driving toward me. Incredibly, and as if in slow motion, the truck landed on the driver's side into the snow-packed ditch. The snow at the top of the incline was even with the top of the driver's side window of my vehicle. It was wedged into the embankment nice and tight, and there was no way I could open the driver's side door to get out. I looked out the passenger's side window as my son's classmate drove by unscathed. As he passed by, he looked at me and waited for a thumbs-up before he continued on his way. I took a moment and thanked God for not hitting him. I was facing the wrong way on a two-way country road. I was okay, but I was not so sure about the truck. Russ was already at work, and I called him to tell him what had happened. He made sure I was all right and then instructed me to call the boys and tell them what had happened and assured me that they would know what to do. When I called Nick and Derrick, they were still home, getting ready for school and told me they would be there as soon as they could. As I waited, I called the high school and let them know that the boys would be there as soon as they helped me out of the ditch. I called work to let them know what happened. I told them I was okay and would let them know if I would be able to drive in or not. As soon as I hung up, Nick and Derrick turned the corner and drove toward me. They backed up their truck as close to my truck as they could. They got out, and I watched them slip and slide on the ice as they made their way to the passenger side of my truck. Happy to see them, I rolled down the passenger's side window, and they asked if I was okay. They explained what they were going to do, and once they were set, all I had to do was steer. I watched in awe as they maneuvered around and got the chains in place to tow me out. They were confident and worked well together. It looked like they had done this a hundred times before. It was obvious they had listened and paid attention to their dad's instructions, and I was impressed and proud. I felt well taken care of at that moment, and I was grateful for their intelligence and their determination. And I was grateful for their love and their caring nature. When they had everything ready, they reminded me that all I had to do was steer as they started to pull the truck out of the ditch.

As they walked back to their truck, I noticed another vehicle in my rearview mirror as it approached from behind me. The vehicle pulled over in front of where I was and parked on the opposite side of the road. My heart sank when I recognized the Jeep and realized it was my dad. It had been four or five years since my parents' withdrawal from my family, and they had had very little to do with my boys for longer than that. My father got out of his truck and approached the boys. I assumed he asked if they needed any help and watched the three of them as they held a short conversation. When I saw my dad raise his hand to say goodbye to my boys, I rolled down the passenger's side window so I could talk to him when he came over to check on me. He walked back to his truck and got in. He never turned in my direction. He never made eye contact with me. He never looked my way or even waved.

Nothing.

He got in his truck and drove away. I don't remember the boys pulling me out. I don't remember driving to work. I was unable to recall the rest of my day. I allowed his actions to numb me, and I remembered other times in my life when I had felt like that. I remembered other times I was invisible. It was a grim reminder that I was not important.

I was on the bleachers, seated in between two friends, preparing to watch my boy's high school basketball game in our hometown. As I looked around, I spotted my mom in the front row, on the floor of the basketball court, and I saw my dad walking around, saying hello to people. They were there to support and cheer on my niece at her basketball game, which would be ending soon.

My mom, although very social, had limited mobility at that point, so she remained near the foot of the bleachers on the court floor. My dad was flitting around in his usual fashion, saying hello to all the folks he knew. I watched as his eyes scoured the upper seats for his next visit. He spotted my good friend Shari seated to my immediate left. My stomach dropped in nervous anticipation as he started walking toward us with his big, welcoming smile. My dad was always on, working the crowd, and making an effort to say hello to everyone he knew. That was his personality—outgoing, happy, and social. He stood in front of me, one row down, with his full attention on Shari. He asked about her mom and dad and cracked jokes and laughed and was his usual cool, charismatic self. He stood there for what I remembered to be an excruciating length of time. He never acknowledged me. He never looked in my direction or made eye contact with me. He was good at ignoring me. He said his goodbyes and headed back to where my mom was seated. When he left, my other friend, Steph, who was seated to my immediate right, leaned over and asked Shari, "Who was *that*?"

Shari stalled uncomfortably, and I interjected by saying, "That was my dad."

Steph leaned back and I observed her confusion as she replayed the conversation and my dad's total lack of acknowledgment toward me. God only knows what else she must have been thinking. Shari was well aware of my situation with my parents, and I wondered what she must have thought about the whole show my dad had just put on. We never spoke of it. I'm sure she knew it embarrassed me and wanted to save me the aggravation of discussing it. Shari and Steph changed the subject and offered me a much-needed distraction from my father's antics. I sat and listened to the squeaky basketball sneakers run, stop, and pivot on the pristine gym floor, as the feelings of shame raced through my head. *Why did he go out of his way to come over just to ignore me? I would have played along and said hi and acted pleasant. Was he afraid that I would respond abrasively, and he didn't want to give me that opportunity? Was he afraid I would embarrass him? No, instead he deliberately chose to single me out and make me feel invisible. Since I was keeping score—swoosh, two points for you, Dad.*

Chapter 6

It's In the Cards

In the spring, a couple of months later, I was invited to a friend's home for an evening of tarot card readings. I accepted the invitation, hoping it would provide some long-anticipated answers for me. The drive to my friend Linda's house was twenty minutes, long enough to get my thoughts in order, questions rehearsed, and skepticism in check. I told myself if nothing else, it would be an affordable evening of entertainment. I've always had an interest in psychic mediums and admired their special gifts and insights. As I drove, I recalled indulging in a guilty pleasure back in my early married life. I watched a television show called *Crossing Over,* where I was mesmerized for an hour of psychic readings given by John Edward. I never shared this particular interest with anyone. I didn't want anyone to know that I believed that someone could communicate with the dead.

I arrived at Linda's house and among a handful of friends were two women who would be conducting the readings. One was dark-haired and short with a gentle, business-like vibe. She was dressed in casual slacks and a floral blouse with a pair of earrings to match. The other

had long, wavy, fair hair and had a go-with-the-flow, hippie vibe.

She wore a floor length skirt and a loose fitting bohemian blouse.

Her bracelets clanked as they moved up and down her arms while

she talked. We shared introductions and had several minutes of

small talk, and then the tarot card readers went to separate rooms

upstairs to begin their work. I decided almost immediately that I

wanted the hippie to do my reading. Although I didn't know what to

call it at the time, I felt a positive energy with her, and it just felt

right. When I entered the room, I was a bit nervous because I had

never experienced a reading before and I didn't know what to

expect. She offered some general information about her gift and then

she asked if I had any particular questions. I asked about my children

and my husband's well-being along with that of my older sister and

her family. As the medium flipped over a few tarot cards, she said,

"Both of your sons are smart and sensitive. They will do well for

themselves in the future."

She asked, "Does your sister have heart trouble?" I offered

that although she may not have a physical ailment with her heart, I believed she had been experiencing emotional heartbreak. The image of the turtle, on the tarot card, was upside down. It had spun over onto its shell with all four feet facing upward. She explained, "Your sister feels upside down regarding some decisions she has made about her children, perhaps this is the heart reference."

She flipped over another card and asked, "Does your husband work for The American Red Cross?" Again, I shook my head, no. The card had a bear on it. She told me that my husband was a good man and she continued, "He is loyal and sweet, with a kind heart. He will help anyone he can and always puts others ahead of himself, making sure that their needs are met before his own. He is honest and hard-working."

The next card she drew had four birds on it and she said, "This symbolizes your family, birds of a feather stick together. You have a strong bond and are tight-knit and will always be there for each other."

I told the medium that I had a question about my mother and father, and she turned another card over, she asked, "Are your parents divorced?"

I told her, "No." She explained, "Although your parents are physically together, they live separate lives. They do not connect and their perfect marriage is a mirage. You are experiencing a role reversal with your parents. Your parents have taken on the role of the child and you have taken on the role of the parent."

Although I hadn't interpreted the shift in our relationship in that way, her evaluation made sense to me. The medium offered an understanding of my relationship with my parents that I had not contemplated. Following that interaction, I asked the question I had been wanting to ask. I was frightened of repeating the pattern of my mother and grandmother.

I asked the medium, "Am I going to lose my relationship and communication with my boys?"

She looked at all the cards laid out in front of her and answered, "No, I don't see that happening here."

That was all I needed to hear and I left the room less worried about an event that felt out of my control. When I started to write this book, I looked back at a detailed list I had made at the time of the reading and discovered that most of what she shared with me had come true. One thing she mentioned that made me question her psychic ability was that she said I would write, and I would travel to Ireland. I giggled to myself, as both of those things were not on my radar, not in the least. She got several things right; but, I have not traveled to Ireland yet.

About six months after my tarot card reading and thirty months of not speaking to my mother, she called me. She invited me to meet for dinner to talk about *things*. The initial phone call made me feel uncomfortable. After I quizzed her a bit more about the parameters of our dinner, I agreed to meet her at a nearby restaurant. Awkward, uneasy, and strange would be a good assessment of our initial greeting. Still unsure and fearing the worst, I imagined an intervention-type atmosphere, picturing family members popping out from behind tables and booths, ready to attack me. After my initial trepidation passed, it was on to the business at hand. I felt my mother's words were well-intentioned, but I heard a lot of, *"Let's forget it and start over."* The conversation was reminiscent of my grandmother and my mother's reconciliation tactics in an attempt to fix their severed relationship. I don't recall an apology or any mention that she missed me or her grandsons. None of what I had yearned for or felt that I needed to hear was addressed. I was cordial and polite. I thanked my mom for dinner and for the opportunity to meet and talk. Upon my departure, I asked that she be patient with Russ and Nick and Derrick and me. I explained that we had spent the last two and a half years getting used to the idea of not having parents or grandparents involved in our lives.

As I drove home, I wondered if she *had* apologized or said she missed me or her grandsons. Perhaps she had and I was too closed off and emotionally deaf to hear it. I realized nothing had changed. The words were nice. The gesture of my mother and me talking was one that I had yearned for and feared. Neither one of us was ready to make a change. We were both stuck, and although we wanted our situation to be better, to be different, I don't believe either one of us knew how to make that happen. Guilt was in the driver's seat and got us to meet, but without true forgiveness, there would be no movement toward reconciliation. Neither one of us had the tools to fix us. I hoped she felt better being able to say what she needed to say. I hoped it helped her release some emotional burdens.

Chapter 7

Fairy Tales

Winged creatures in sets of three represent important spirits in my life. Their visits bring an immediate sense of peace and calm. A new energy washes over me as I watch butterflies, geese, and birds flutter around me.

I stand at the window, clutching my coffee, allowing the aroma to fill my senses while I gaze at the three doves hovering around the bird feeder.

They reinforce a feeling that everything will be okay.

As I stood gazing out the window, clutching onto a lukewarm memory and a hot coffee mug, my thoughts transported me back to November 2009. A melancholy sense of what could have been washed over me as I recalled the speech I had rehearsed in my head for years. I planned on toasting my parents while singing their praises at their golden anniversary party, but I never uttered one word of it.

I remembered how different things had gone at the actual celebration. I was invited, much to my surprise, but I guess we can all act like everything is okay for a couple of hours. My older sister, Kelly, and my niece Allison came over to my house before the anniversary party. I opened a bottle of wine to toast our time together, but mostly to help soften the edges before seeing my parents. Kelly and Allison's warm hearts combined with a chilled glass of wine gave me the courage I needed to attend the event.

There were many family members and friends in attendance whom I hadn't seen in years. I sensed most of the folks were oblivious to our falling out, which confused me. *Were people being polite, or did they honestly not know?* I sat and ate and mingled with a few people. I wanted to cry, thinking of the changes that had taken place that no longer allowed me to want to sing my parents' praises in the speech I wouldn't be giving. *Welcome, family and friends . . . blah, blah blah.*

I remembered how I believed in the life of that happy young girl being chased in the sand by her dad, her hero. I remembered how I believed in the life of that fun girl who learned to dance with her mom in the living room. I remembered how I believed in the life of that smart girl whose school work was praised. I remembered how I believed in the life of that curious girl who watched and learned from her mom, with admiration. I remembered how I believed in the life of that sleepy girl who was cradled in protective arms and read to from a giant book of fairy tales. I missed that girl, and I missed that mom and dad.

MY SOUL CONTRACT

Chapter 8

Silence is Golden

My heartache was as deep as a canyon, bearing the weight of betrayal and hurt. My tormented will had collapsed beneath a knowing. There were no right words and no way to repair the damage. If I thought I struggled before, it would be nothing compared to what I was about to feel. The storm had just begun.

It was a Friday afternoon, May, 2010 and I had just checked into my hotel room when my cell phone rang. It was my sister Kelly. She apologized for poor timing but her important news couldn't wait. She called to tell me that my mom had been diagnosed with leukemia. Kelly filled me in on my mom's prognosis and treatment options and informed me that my mom was scheduled to undergo aggressive treatment the following day. I asked my sister to keep me posted as I was not due home from my business trip in Orlando until

Sunday evening. I hung up the phone and began to research the blood cancer known as leukemia.

As I gathered the facts, I struggled with my role. *Should I stay in Orlando or head home?* After a sleepless night of deliberation, I figured there was not much I could do while my mom was having treatment, so I decided to stay in Orlando. Saturday was a busy workday, and the busy day was followed by dinner and entertainment. When the entertainment concluded, I advised my coworker of my mother's circumstances and excused myself to go back to my hotel room. I called Kelly to ask how my mother's scheduled treatment went. The news was not good. The treatment was so aggressive that my mother suffered a stroke. I reminded my sister that I would be home Sunday, and on Monday morning I needed to drive to southern Illinois to pick Nick up from college and bring him home for the summer.

I had so many things going on and so many feelings to sort through. The hurt, abandoned daughter part of me felt unattached and separated. That disconnection supported the thought that staying away was okay. The caring, sympathetic daughter part of me thought I should go to the hospital to be with my mom. A case of guilt supported the thought of leaving Orlando, but guilt also kept me there to fulfill my work role. I decided to ask my sister for guidance, as I was not sure if I would be a welcome visitor at the hospital with my family. Kelly assured me that whatever I decided, she would accept and understand my position. I decided to stay, and when Sunday arrived, I was so anxious to get home that I didn't even care that I hated the thought of flying.

Thought of getting back home to Russ and Derrick, holding my sweet eight-week-old kitten, Blue, and the excitement of getting Nick back home for the summer, was enough to take my mind off of the flight and my mom's ill health.

Our plane landed in Chicago, and a limo was waiting to drive my coworkers and me back to the office, where we had left our cars. Exhausted and anxious to get home, we said our goodbyes and loaded our luggage into our vehicles. I called Russ while I let the car warm up to let him know I would be home in thirty minutes. During our short conversation, I sensed there was something wrong, and I questioned Russ about it. He said that we would talk about it when I got home.

When I pulled into the driveway and pressed the garage door opener, I noticed, in the middle of the garage floor, the cat carrier and Blue's food and water bowls. While still seated in my car I noticed, through the open mudroom door, that the room appeared to be emptied out. I could not put the pieces together. I wondered what had happened and why Blue wasn't in the mudroom. I got out of my car and stood inside the mudroom only to verify my suspicions. It was obvious Russ had cleaned the carpet. *Maybe Blue was in the house?* I went inside and was greeted by our exuberant, sweet lab, Ratchet and loved him up and greeted him with my usual, "Hi, baby." Then I went into the living room, where my husband and son were.

I asked, "What's wrong? Where is Blue?"

My husband got up and held out his arms. I went in for a long hug. I started crying because I already knew what he was struggling to tell me. Russ was so upset that he could hardly speak. He told me that he had gone out that morning to feed Blue, and he was just lying there. He knew right away he was gone. Russ searched everywhere and cleaned every inch of the mudroom to see if Blue had gotten into something that caused him to die, but Russ found nothing.

I cried myself to sleep that night as I allowed the sudden loss of Blue, the impact of my mother's ill health, and the emotional reunion I would have with Nick the next morning envelop me.

After a restless night, I got up early to make the ninety-minute drive to Nick's college. While I drove, I granted myself permission to feel the elevated emotions of the much-anticipated reunion with my eldest son to rise above the unpleasantness that was going on.

As I pulled up along the curb near the dorms, I noticed, in true Nick fashion, he was already outside with all of his belongings, waiting for me. I was overjoyed to see him. I couldn't park and open my door fast enough to run across the street and give him a long, anticipated hug. I released my embrace and looked into his eyes, truly grateful for his presence. Without warning, a tear welled up in my eyes. He asked me, "What's wrong, Mom?"

"I am so happy to see you!"

"No, Mom, I know something is wrong. What is it?"

Well, crap, I thought I would be able to pull this off and have a happy reunion moment. I've never been good at disguising my true feelings. I could never hide anything from my boys. They are too smart and too perceptive about life and always have been. I tried to deliver the sad news about Blue, which would have been much harder for my son to hear than his grandmother's health diagnosis. I was an emotional mess while I explained everything that had happened over the past forty-eight hours.

We drove home together, chatty and quiet and emotional. Russ and Derrick welcomed Nick home when we arrived later that morning. We all worked together, excited to get Nick's things unloaded and downstairs to his bedroom so he could get moved back in as soon as possible. We had just finished the last load to Nick's downstairs bedroom and, as I made my way to the top of the stairs, the house phone rang, and caller ID told me it was my sister Kelly. She told me that my mom was worse and that her doctor and nurses were discussing DNR options with my dad. He requested that the four of us discuss the options and make those decisions together.

For nearly a decade, I had longed for our reconciliation. The wait for that was emotionally and physically exhausting, and I had accepted that my mom and dad and I would never connect how we once had. The light of my once undeniable grasp of deep affection and loyalty had been extinguished over the last several years. I had anticipated the reality of what was now inevitable. I had come to terms with the fact that one of my parents would become ill, and it would be that illness that would force us together.

With my stomach in knots, the twisted, sour reality of our circumstances hindered my gait as I walked along the hospital corridor. My legs were weak and my hands trembled as I approached my mom's hospital room doorway. Tears started to well up as I got closer. I squelched the feeling and reminded myself to be strong. I opened the door and saw my mom lying in her hospital bed. As I made my way toward her and stood at the foot of her bed, our eyes met, and when she recognized me, a smile spread evenly across her face.

It was then that I experienced *the look*. I will never forget that look, and I will forever hold it in my heart. The stroke had stolen her speech, but the look said everything that needed to be said in one moment for all time. It was a familiar look I had witnessed before, a look of relief and gratitude. I felt her warm breath in my ear as if she were standing right beside me. *Oh you're here, I am so happy to see you, thank you for coming. I love you. I am sorry.*

The next couple of days were rough. I continued to go to work and used my lunch hour to travel ten minutes to the hospital, check on my mother's condition, share thirty-five awkward minutes with family, and use the remaining time to get back to work.

It was decided amongst the four of us that my dad would sign a Do Not Resuscitate order.

A full workweek had passed since I had returned from Orlando, and some friends had invited me to join them for dinner and a movie. I was excited to laugh and relax with my dear friends and I welcomed a much-needed distraction from work and my mom's health issues. But as I walked toward my car, my phone began to ring and it was Kelly. She told me that my mom was not doing well and hospice wanted to meet with the family. I canceled my plans and headed over to the hospital. I arrived in my mom's hospital room, and what I saw felt uncomfortable and familiar. I glanced toward the nurse's station and was relieved to see one of the nurses I recognized from an earlier visit, on duty. I needed to ask her some questions. I had experience in this from nine years earlier with my dear father-in-law. He had battled lung cancer and was victorious for a few years, but, the long-term effects of chemotherapy and radiation damaged his heart beyond repair. Dad Abels's last days were spent under hospice care. It was through that experience that I learned about the stages the human body goes through at the end of life. I learned a great deal from the incredible hospice nurses and learned what questions to ask based on my experiences during that time.

The hospice representative had not arrived yet, so I asked my family to excuse me for a moment. I asked the familiar nurse if I could speak with her for a moment. I prefaced what I was about to ask with the fact that I was a straight shooter and that I didn't want any information to be sugarcoated. Then I asked the nurse, "Can you tell me about my mother's prognosis?"

The nurse replied, "I respect your approach and your mom's prognosis is not good. She doesn't have much time left. We are trying to keep her as comfortable as possible."

Knowing that night would probably be my mom's last, I joined my sisters and my dad, in the waiting area, where the hospice representative was waiting to meet with us. The hospice person introduced herself and started talking about options for my mother's immediate care. I observed as my dad became fidgety and animated in his responses, a familiar reaction when he was uncomfortable and tense. I listened as my sisters asked questions that pertained to my mom's long-term care. My family seemed confused by the meeting and were scared and not ready to accept our difficult situation, or they were oblivious to the seriousness of my mom's condition.

I remained quiet during most of the discussion with the hospice representative. I paid attention to what she was saying but even more attention to my dad's and sisters' reactions. It was clear to me that my family did not understand my mom's grave condition. I decided it was time to ask, "What do we need to do to prepare ourselves?"

The hospice nurse turned toward me and said, "I am so glad you asked that question, it is very important."

I could tell by her body language and her eye contact with me that she knew I understood my mother's condition. I wasn't sure if my interjection felt easy because I had been removed from my family for so long or if it was easy because I had gone through a similar event with my father-in-law. At that point, however, I didn't feel like dancing around the truth, and it became necessary for me to play the role of the no-crap-allowed fact finder. I felt I needed to shine a light on the seriousness of my mother's condition, and I couldn't sit and witness my family's confusion and denial any longer.

Just then a nurse entered the waiting area and instructed us to go to my mom's room. As we entered, the nurse told us that my mom wouldn't have much longer. There were no words spoken between us. There was a simple understanding. We each took turns holding my mom's hand, crying, and saying our goodbyes. I was last, and I leaned over to whisper in my mom's ear. I didn't want anyone else to hear what I was about to say. I felt so vulnerable and small and helpless.

I said, "I don't understand what happened between us, and I am sorry for the pain I caused. I hope you can forgive me. I forgive you and I love you, and if you need to go, it's okay."

I stood up and felt that I should leave my post. I felt that I didn't deserve to be right next to my mom, holding her hand. It shouldn't be me. It should have been one of my sisters, perhaps one she was closer to, but I couldn't move. I gave her a kiss on her cheek and remembered how soft it felt, and as I stood up I heard my mom take what would be her last breath.

As the nurses removed whatever apparatus was still connected to her, I tried to comprehend what I had just witnessed. It was so peaceful and quiet and oddly beautiful. We were all there, just how she would have hoped. We all had an opportunity to say what we needed to say. There was muffled crying and deep sadness, guilt, and powerlessness. A peaceful surrender occurred. I realized in that moment how complex and brittle and fast life is. In one moment someone was here, alive, and breathing, and in the next moment they were not. Intellectually, I knew that, but it all felt very surreal. Very odd, as if I expected more chaos but instead I experienced a simple and peaceful reality. There was no fight, just a powerful acceptance as her body decided it was time to let go. I thought about who was waiting for her on the other side. Her mom and dad, her Uncle Bob, her grandma, and all of her pets and all of our family pets. She would like that the most, I think. It brought me comfort to picture her reuniting with all of them.

I thought about my dad and how lost he would be without his love of more than fifty years. I thought about my younger sister and the close companion she had just lost. I thought about my older sister and the role model, friend, and wonderful mother she had just lost. I cried years earlier when I lost my mom to our estrangement. The tears I cried that night were for my family. Bearing witness to their loss was more painful than my own.

Robotically, we all made our way out of the hospital. I don't recall who went with whom, but I do know I was all alone. As I drove myself past my folk's house, I didn't turn in the driveway. I hadn't been inside their house in years. I felt as though I had been locked out of this place, their home, and their hearts. We had danced the same dance for years. I was waiting for them to lead, and they were waiting for me to lead. We were stuck in an upside-down world filled with chaos and uncertainty. I glanced up their driveway as I drove past. I would have felt like an unwelcome guest, and I was sure I was the last person my dad would have wanted consoling him. I had relinquished those roles a long time ago.

I received my mother's stroke as a gift. It took her voice, which had dominated for so long, and for once we were both able to listen. We were able to share our hearts during her last moments.

If I thought I struggled before my mom's death, it would be nothing compared to what I was about to feel. The storm had just begun. I spent the next several months feeling the impact of losing my mother along with our unspoken truths and a laundry list of internal battles that bubbled to the surface begging for answers.

Chapter 9

Sword and Shield

Holding a sword in one hand and a shield in the other, I defend the sacred space located just behind my breastbone. I am a warrior both courageous and afraid. I want to trust but at what cost? I want to let down my walls, but it feels like a disloyal action against the architect. Lowering my protective gear makes me far too vulnerable for attack, but I am weary for the fight. My body is tired and my arms ache while vigilantly shepherding my flock. My spirit begs my mind and body for respite.

My heart yearns for safety, openness, and vulnerability.

It began one evening as I drove home from work. I arrived in my driveway so mechanically that I couldn't recall if I had stopped at all the stop signs or if I had been aware of any vehicles I may have passed along the way. I was deep inside my head, marinating in my repetitive thoughts. *What had distracted my thoughts so much that I couldn't remember my drive home?* I was so bothered by the distraction that I sat in my driveway and began to trace my thoughts backward. I started with the last thought I recalled. *Got it. What made me think of that? And what did I think right before that thought?* And so on. As I sat and traced back my thoughts, it became clear to me that I had spent the last several months repeating the same dialogue over and over in my head. I realized in my quiet moments that all I thought about was the derailed relationship with my parents. I replayed the hurt and pain of how our relationship ended, as a constant loop in my thoughts. Our toxic patterns of behavior had woven their way into the depths of my being, and I allowed them to affect all of my relationships. I had become a crabby mom, a bitchy wife, and a whiny friend. I did, however, have a new job where I could pretend that everything was normal for at least forty hours between Monday and Friday.

For some reason, on this particular day, not being able to recall my drive home bothered me enough to do some inner investigation. It made me realize just how distracted I had been. I started to review how my experience with my parents had changed me. On one hand, I felt numb and detached, with no resources or skills to help fix the emotional damage. On the other hand, I remained capable of feeling every ounce of guilt and shame associated with the enormity of our separation. I needed to sort out my feelings. I needed to develop some skills to help me understand all of it. I was intrigued to dig as deep as necessary to discover the answers and bring some peace and understanding into my life. I was angry and tired, and tired of being angry and tired. I had to figure out how to release my burdens.

After thoughtful deliberation, I decided that I needed to have a conversation with the people who had hurt me. The most immediate and most necessary person was my dead mother. To have shared that thought with anyone would have felt a bit silly, but so many things were left unsaid between us. I was holding on to so much anger that I felt I needed a private space to talk and to have a good cry. I decided to have the conversation in the most alluring place in my yard.

Russ is quite handy and can build just about anything, and he built the most eye-pleasing and tranquil space in our yard. A comfortable space for entertaining, with ample seating around a built-in fire pit. In each corner of the patio are flowering ornamental trees that boast a light-pink bloom each spring. At the north end of the patio are three separate flower beds with mature perennials and a variety of vibrantly colored annuals, which invite melodic songbirds to share our quiet retreat. And because we live in the country, I wouldn't need to be concerned about neighbors listening in on my one-sided, slightly demented conversation with my dead mother.

It happened to be a perfect Saturday spring morning, and the sun was shining and the birds were singing. I sat in my favorite chair and settled in. I felt strange and awkward as I began.

"Hi, Mom. I wondered if we could have a conversation. Well, I guess it's more me talking, saying what I didn't get to say to you before you died. I felt kind of cheated about that, I am angry with you. I need to tell you why, and I need you to hear me. I am not saying these things to hurt you. I am saying these things because there is something at work here urging me to let these thoughts and these negative feelings go. I have been hanging on to all of these feelings for too long."

I started with the pain of feeling abandoned after the store debacle. I shared the hurt that I felt surrounding my children and

Russ. The more I talked, the more I was able to recall even more pain. Events from my childhood came up. The more I talked, the more I remembered. I laid it all out. More hurt. More pain. I yelled. I sobbed. I felt a huge release. I felt she heard me and I began to feel better. I experienced several moments of clarity. Each time I recalled an impactful memory of hurt and betrayal, I connected it to an equally emotional event from my childhood. I recalled being laughed at because I was sensitive. I remembered being curious and feeling like my questions were unimportant. I recalled the memory of moving out of my parent's house before Russ and I got married. I remembered how they ignored me as I made several trips back and forth, loading boxes into my car. I passed by carrying my things while my mom watched television and my dad read the newspaper. They didn't say one word to me. I remembered wondering if they were mad at me. I sat for a long time and allowed myself to recall everything in my memory that felt significant in that moment. I watched as if a movie were playing in front of me while I experienced vivid clarity. This repeated over and over, and it felt so strange, yet so healing. I felt as if I were not in control of what was happening—oddly, it progressed on its own. Instead of steering, I was a passenger being shown things I hadn't thought about in years. More clarity. More healing. This went on for a very long time. I don't recall how long I was in the garden with my mom, but I knew when it was done. I knew by the exhaustion I felt and the final release of tears that I was done. The sitting, the talking, and the connection was done for the day. I was physically and emotionally spent. As the experience progressed, I felt instructed to surrender. Once I surrendered, I experienced an enormous amount of clarity.

There was a shift in energy, and the release of my tears marked each shift. I learned by talking out loud that all the pain and emotion I had been holding on to were directly connected to earlier childhood events. The pain mirrored validation from earlier experiences, and the clarity I experienced answered some of my questions. It felt like a very deep internal understanding. I felt contentment in my heart. I felt support unlike anything I had experienced in my life. I felt as though I had been given a map to my heart.

As the day went on, I was able to examine my experiences and compare them with past experiences and recognize the similarities. I realized how I had been holding on to the memories of those experiences and how I had been behaving from a place of hurt. I also realized my innate tendency throughout my life had been to pull away. A pattern of behavior for me was to say something hurtful, cut off my communication, and retreat into silence. This was how I punished the people I cared about. An observed behavior from my parents that I had learned to mimic. If someone hurt me, my defensive walls would come up, and my ego, in defense of my feelings, held a protective shield in front of my heart.

I gained a resourceful tool in the garden with my mom, and because of that I knew I had much more work to do. I decided that I would create a healing toolbox of sorts. My toolbox would help me examine the process of how I had found the answers during my conversation in the garden with my mom. My toolbox contains questions and an illusory hammer and chisel to chip away at the mortar that held the walls of my stories together.

On that spring day, I vowed to honor a commitment to do the work of dismantling my skillfully constructed walls brick by brick. One question in the toolbox is, *how is this experience similar to another time you felt like this?*

I trusted that the answers would come. I simply had to ask and do the work. The work was to recall the emotion attached to the event and continue digging to uncover other events in my life that were emotionally relatable. I had an inner wisdom directing me to connect with my childhood. I knew that if I felt left out as an adult, the work, the digging through the protective wall to find the event that initially made the child version of me feel left out would be the key to my healing.

I felt as if I had been reborn. I knew in a sense I had. I felt as if I had a relationship with something greater than I was. There was a higher energy that took possession of my thoughts and my heart. I felt guided, supported, and loved. I had always believed in something higher, a divine energy that saturates everyone and everything with love. Some may call this divine energy God or Source or the Universe. After my experience in the garden that Saturday, I felt an obligation to thank somebody or something— angels, my mom, the Universe, all of it. Overwhelmed with gratitude, I asked for continued guidance through this process, whatever that might be. I prayed for a difference, an understanding of what felt like a strong spiritual connection. I prayed that I may be blessed with angelic advocates that would help steer the course as I vowed to navigate the uncharted waters that lay ahead of me.

Now that I had had what turned out to be the first of many substantial conversations with my dead mother, I felt it was time to have a conversation with my still-very-much-alive father. A conversation I anticipated to be much more difficult. I thought about the rotten daughter I had been—justified, but rotten. I was torn, as a part of me felt rational about my decision not to pursue a relationship after my folks quit speaking to me, but the other part of me felt ashamed for not pursuing any relationship at all. A part of me felt almost embarrassed when I thought about the face-to-face conversation I would have with my dad. I felt like a disloyal daughter when I pictured his sad face turning my pain into his pain.

Each time I thought about talking with my dad, shame pulled me back to where I didn't want to be. Pain fueled my intentions to have a conversation with my dad by recalling how my boys had been treated. I needed to have the conversation for them. I was able to keep the hurt very much alive by reminding myself that not only was I not important enough to have a relationship with, but my parent's grandsons were also not important enough. I was tired of carrying the burden of my family's combined hurt and resentment around with me every minute of every day. If I was to have my intended conversation with my dad, I would need time to get my thoughts in order and my heart prepared. I would need time as I attempted to extract some compassion for myself and some understanding for my dad. My dad doesn't handle uncomfortable things well, and he has always had a short attention span. Attempting to have a serious conversations with him was like trying to have a grown-up conversation with a four-year-old hyped up on sugar.

I prepared my heart as I rehearsed my conversation and pictured my dad's reaction as a combination of sadness and lighthearted distraction of deeply ingrained denial. I prepared myself for what I had known my whole life, yet I wanted the exact opposite to happen. I didn't think my dad would take responsibility for his role in our separation, but I hoped I might extract a different reaction from him.

Teaching Moment: Not one of us is without the experience of pain. We experience pain at different levels at a young age. Our ego, protective in its nature, will defend the initial wound. The wound that was created by a negative experience may lay untouched for a very long time. The ego stands at attention, ready to react, using any means possible to protect the open wound. The wound is considered open, festering, and raw because it has not healed and causes inner pain. We become well-rehearsed in protecting our wounds, and our ego is the unconscious defender. Ego dons its warrior gear, sword in hand, and defends the wounds.

When I found the answers, as I had on that Saturday morning talking with my mom, tears validated an inner shift, and I experienced a breakthrough. I realized that if I made a conscious effort to do the work, the answers would follow. I wondered if it could be that simple. It was a foreign concept for me to take ownership and understand that it was going to be an internal battle to discover my authentic self. I spoke my mind and my truth to my parents once, and it didn't end well. This time it felt different and invigorating. There was an immeasurable amount of light beaming through my body, my mind, and my soul.

Chapter 10

Vacation for Two

While the trepidation of the impending talk with my dad loomed overhead, Russ approached me with an idea for the two of us to take a fall vacation. I assessed the following before I answered. *Ever since our boys were born, we've never taken a vacation without them, and that would feel strange.* I reminded myself that they were not kids anymore and were capable of taking care of themselves and handling their own affairs. Derrick lived at home and would be able to take care of the house and our pets, and I had vacation time at work, so I said, "Sure, that will be fun."

Russ then added, "I think it would be even better if we took two weeks!"

"All at once?"

Russ laughed. "Yeah, all at once."

I began to resist the idea of being gone for two weeks. Panicked, I listed the reasons why a two-week vacation would not work. Russ listened as I rattled off part of my list.

Feeling overwhelmed, I imagined the pile of work that would be waiting for me when I returned and the drowning feeling of not being able to catch up. I began to feel as if a two-week vacation was not worth the hassle.

"First of all, I am not sure if I can take off two consecutive weeks from work. That's an awful lot to ask of my coworkers."

Russ suggested, "Let the idea sink in a little, give it some thought, and we'll discuss it later. We have time to decide. Okay?"

Thinking about it provided more time to think about more reasons not to go. At the top of my list of reasons not to go was the biggest one of all and the one I had not shared with Russ. *What in the hell are the two of us going to do for fourteen days together?* The reality was that we hadn't been alone on vacation together in over twenty years. It had always been our choice. We never even thought about taking a vacation without our kids.

Frazzled, I began with the self-talk. *If I remove the kids as the primary focus on vacation that leaves just us. If I'm brutally honest, it's been so long, I don't even remember how to act all alone. Well, yes, the obvious thing that couples do when they are alone but we can't have sex all day, every day. What the heck will we talk about? We don't have any shared hobbies. I mean, we both like the water and the boat and fishing and eating, but then what? What if we find out we don't even like each other after this?* Russ let me have a week to think about it before he brought it up again.

"Well, have you thought more about vacation?"

"I just don't know, hon, it's a long time," I offered.

I started with my list of reasons why not. He let me go on and get myself all worked up, and then he came over right in front of me. He put his hands on my shoulders and asked, "What are you afraid of?"

God, that man knows me! Too well sometimes. I couldn't lie, he had locked eyes with me. He would have known if I made up something, so I had to blurt it out. Ashamed to share my insecure thoughts, I started to cry a little.

"Russ, I'm afraid we will run out of things to do. We haven't been without the kids in so long. What if we don't even like each other anymore?"

Russ laughed and said, "Well, then I guess we will find out." He assured me that we would find plenty to keep us busy. I asked him point blank, "What things are we going to do?"

"Well, we could go to the antique shops there."

He had given this some thought, and I was impressed that he was thinking outside of the usual vacation box. I had to laugh a little because we had never talked about antique shopping before, and part of me wondered, *Who are you, and what have you done with my husband?* Still feeling that he had to prove to me that we could fill up two weeks' worth of free time, I reluctantly agreed.

"Ooookayy, I guess it will be fine; we'll go for two weeks."

We experienced two weeks of relaxed relationship bliss in the fall of 2014 on our beloved Norfork Lake in Arkansas. We did what we wanted to do when we wanted to do it. For the first time in a long time, there was no schedule. Russ and I did some antique shopping and discovered we had a new shared interest. Russ went fishing in the mornings, and I slept in late. We spent lazy afternoons sitting on the patio reading or just relaxing. Sometimes I cooked but more often we dined out. We spent some afternoons on the water and every evening on the lake. Sometimes we fished and sometimes we just relaxed and talked. Each evening promised a captivating sunset that seemed to get better as we breathed in the peaceful landscape.

One evening, after a couple glasses of wine, as we gazed at the gorgeous sunset, I felt comfortable enough to talk to Russ about my recent decision to have a conversation with my dad. I knew that Russ was content leaving things just as they were. Russ is a man who makes his decisions and is good with those decisions, seldom changing his mind. I have never known him to second-guess himself. His confidence and his morals were two of the many things that attracted me to him so many years ago. I knew that suggesting opening things up with my dad would be a sensitive subject because of the pain my parents caused, particularly to our boys.

Russ has been protecting me since I was sixteen years old, and he will continue to protect me and his boys for as long as he lives. By broaching the subject, I would be kicking up some old crap that Russ had tucked away for good.

I asked Russ if he would mind if I talked about my dad. I started by telling him that I had been thinking about our situation and how it had made me feel.

I explained, "I can't hold on to the bitterness and anger any longer and there's a part of me that has a hard time wanting to talk with my dad because it feels like a betrayal to you and the boys. I've felt for so long that I needed to carry the torch for all of us. I understand that you needed to work through your part of all of this on your own terms and the boys need to work through their experience on their own terms. I feel ready to have a conversation with my dad and I want to tell him that I'm sorry and that I've forgiven him and my mom."

Russ listened and understood my views and in a sense gave me his blessing to let go of the torch I had been carrying and to pursue whatever I felt I needed to with my dad.

"Whatever it is you feel you need to do, I will support you. I understand that you feel you need to do this, but I hope you are not asking me to join you. I have not changed the way I feel. I can't forgive what your mom and dad did. I can't forgive them for hurting you, and I certainly can't forgive them for hurting our boys. I will wait for an apology from your dad. I will wait for an apology from him to Nick and Derrick. Until that happens, I will not be speaking with him or forgiving him."

I was not surprised by Russ's response. I knew he felt the same way as he had several years earlier. I set my wineglass down and allowed my body to sink into my husband's chest. His arms wrapped around me as I felt the tension leave my body. He kissed my cheek and rested his head on my shoulder. I caressed his strong arms and cried a sweet release of pent-up emotions. I felt as though I could breathe again. I wished I could fix this for all of us. But, Russ was right, I couldn't fix it for him or the boys.

I was proud of myself for taking the opportunity to speak my truth and be vulnerable with my husband. I had been holding on to all of the angst surrounding my mom's death and whatever relationship could be salvaged with my dad for so long. I was able to give myself permission to move forward.

As I sat alone later, I started to think of the impact my father's beliefs had had on me growing up. Although I now know them to be his insecurities, I absorbed his beliefs like a good little sponge. My father was very concerned with appearance. He always told my sisters and me that when we left the house we should always look presentable. He'd remind us, "You might see someone you haven't seen in a long time. Make sure your hair and makeup are done and that you are dressed nicely."

As I sipped my wine and we strolled back to the dock, I drifted back to 1981. It was the October following my high school graduation when Russ and I took a trip to Ruidoso, New Mexico. We borrowed my parents' motorcycle and met my family at one of the biggest motorcycle rallies held there annually.

After our first day of travel, Russ and I checked into our hotel room for the night. Exhausted, I brushed my teeth, removed my makeup, took a shower, and got ready for bed. I guess it hadn't occurred to me that Russ had never seen me without makeup, but when I came out of the bathroom he took one look at me and said, "Whoa."

The look on his face was priceless. I said, "What?"

Russ said, "I guess I've never seen you without makeup."

I felt self-conscious, and I remembered what my dad had taught me. I wondered if that was why I always believed I shouldn't go without makeup. My insecurity spoke loud and clear. *Wouldn't want to scare anyone away. I guess Dad was right.*

That memory brought up another one from 1983. My mom and I were babysitting my five-month-old nephew. I was in the shower, and my mother asked if she could hand Adam to me and bathe him while I was in there. I agreed because I knew it would save time getting ready for the day. After all, I am sure my mom had to get her hair and makeup done too. Soapy, slippery babies are very difficult to maneuver in the shower, and I feared several times that I might drop him. I decided it would be easier if I lathered him up while resting him on my hip. As I turned him around, I held him out to give him a big smile and reassure him that I would never drop him. He took one look at me and became frightened and began to cry. He was so upset, he started shaking, and I couldn't settle him down. I had to yell for my mom to come get him because I could not soothe him.

My mom determined that it must have startled him to see me with wet hair and no makeup. We figured even though I sounded like Aunt Micki, I sure didn't look like Aunt Micki. I felt bad that I had given the poor baby the shock of his lifetime. We laughed about it later, but I couldn't help but think *Dad was right.*

After wandering down memory lane and arriving at the boat dock, I realized that to this day, I do not take my makeup off before bed. Some things are drilled in and hard to release. I thought of the façade I accepted and how the importance of outward appearance during my formative years was an extreme priority. It was more important to portray an image than to be natural. While other dads were begging their daughters not to wear makeup, mine was making sure we didn't leave home without it.

I realized that the priorities instilled in me as an impressionable young girl proved that outside appearances were very important. As long as everything looked good on the outside, everything was okay. I thought about how my perception and my perspective were molded on these beliefs. I thought about what I was brought up to believe in, and I began to question whether or not these beliefs were as comfortable as they once were.

I noticed I was much more relaxed since I had shared my intentions of talking to my dad with Russ. I experienced a release that invited memories from my childhood. Later, on vacation, I was able to recall some fond, feel-good memories that had been suppressed for a long time. Spending the last few years feeling bitter about my circumstances had not allowed many good memories of my mom and dad to surface.

On our drive home after our vacation together, I thanked Russ for talking me into going on a two-week vacation. I was grateful that he was patient with me and that he knew me well enough to address my fears and asked me to share. I confided to Russ that from now on, I wanted all of our vacations to be two weeks long! He laughed and rolled his eyes at me.

When we returned home from vacation, I wrote my dad a letter that I would hand-deliver and ask him to read in my presence. I knew I would not be able to get through what I needed to say without choking up. No matter how much I rehearsed the words, I didn't trust myself to get through his emotional detours. I never knew for sure if my mom had shared with my dad the last conversation she and I had. There were so many things I wanted to explain and discuss. I wanted to take my time and make sure I chose my words sensitively. The letter offered an opportunity for me to make sure he knew what that conversation was all about. In the letter I addressed the main topics and shared my viewpoints. I wanted to convey that my intention was to improve our relationship. I needed to be clear that if he wanted to have a relationship with Russ, Nick, or Derrick, he would need to apologize and address them individually. I didn't want him to mistake our meeting as a cure-all that included my husband or my kids. I explained that I believed all of us had made decisions that resulted in our separation and that we each shared a certain responsibility. I wanted to tell my dad that I loved him and that I had forgiven him.

When I was satisfied with my letter, I called my dad to ask if I could visit. We agreed on a date and time, and before I knew it, I was waiting for him to answer a door I had never been expected to knock on before. I was nervous about seeing my dad and apprehensive about my letter. He opened the door and I don't remember if we hugged or not. We made small talk, and it felt formal as he offered me coffee. We took our coffee into the front room, and we made polite conversation. My dad sat across from me, and when the conversation moved past the weather, I told him that I had a letter I would like him to read.

I set my coffee cup down and brought it over to him. He took the envelope from me and set it on the table beside him. I had not anticipated that, and it was too awkward to try to fill the quiet with uncomfortable conversation, so I asked him, "Dad, would you mind reading that while I'm here?"

He agreed, and as he opened the envelope, I could feel my heart pound inside my chest. My hands clenched the tepid mug as I watched and listened as he chose to read part of the letter aloud. He read and nodded, as if in agreement, and he cried. I cried. When he was finished, he folded the letter and put it back in the envelope.

"Thank you."

I smiled and said, "I have something that I need to say. I have forgiven you and mom for what happened. Can you forgive me?"

With tears in his eyes, he nodded his head yes. I set my coffee cup down and went to my dad and we hugged. It was a nice, long hug, one I had missed.

It was an emotional afternoon, and I was grateful to have the opportunity to sit with my dad and share what needed to be shared.

I felt that we could begin a new relationship and it could be whatever

it was supposed to be.

Chapter 11

Memorials and Jewelry

Several months passed with intermittent phone calls and preannounced visits with my dad. I would never have popped in unexpectedly like I used to; that would have felt strange for both of us. During one of my visits, I was more relaxed and able to focus a bit more on the things in my dad's house. As I looked around, I noticed how nothing had changed. Everything was as I remembered it, just as my mom had left it. A few things appeared to have changed in the kitchen except for the shrine dedicated to my sister's family that lived on all visible sides of the refrigerator. Front and center were pictures of her kids, newspaper clippings about their business, and stuff I couldn't bring myself to investigate because that pissed me off.

It had always pissed me off.

My dad never liked to cook. He would say, "I can't stand to eat or look at anything I cooked."

I guess he had to learn to do both. I noticed my mom and dad's fiftieth wedding anniversary picture on the dining room table.

The table my mom so treasured, didn't seem to be used for family dinners anymore. It had become more of a desk with books and bills and paperwork spread over the top of it. I noticed the pictures on the mantle above the fireplace and the ones that hung above it on the wall. One of my favorite pictures was an 11" x 14" of all eight grandkids (at the time), that my sisters and I presented to my folks as a Christmas gift. We copied a theme I had used with my own kids' professional portraits. They boys were barefoot, and bare-chested, wearing nothing but bib overalls. The girls were barefoot and tucked in a white shirt beneath their bib overalls. Each grandchild had a red bandana tucked in the rear pocket. The bandanas were a smaller version of the red bandanas my dad always had in his pocket and used as a handkerchief. My mom had sewn smaller ones for the kids to have so they could be just like Bup. I loved that picture and the fun we had planning that special gift.

When I visited my dad, I remained in the kitchen and sometimes moved to the living room. Feeling more like a guest than a family member, I had no reason to venture into any other areas of my dad's home. As I sat in the living room, I noticed a few pictures had been updated of my nieces and nephews since the last time I had seen them, but the rest of the knickknacks and decorations seemed to be right where my mom had left them.

It was a good visit. It wasn't too awkward, as my dad and I seemed to be getting more comfortable with whatever the new dynamic of our relationship was. As I drove the short two-mile distance back home, my thoughts drifted back to my mom's memorial service. She wanted to be cremated, and we honored her wishes and held a memorial service at the community shelter in our town. It was a good-sized gathering, and I saw old friends and distant family members separated by miles and time. I remembered how wonderful it felt to see the people that made me recall my youth. Many I knew from our motorcycle days and from our old neighborhood. The deep-seated nostalgic feelings of those friends moved me to tears. Tears for the good people and the good times I so desperately missed. They were simple days spent with my family, and a great deal of that time was spent traveling together because of the family business.

Mom and Dad started their business selling custom-made leather garments in the mid-1970s. My mother had learned to sew from her mother and used her exceptional seamstress abilities early on to upholster furniture and make wedding gowns. There wasn't much she couldn't sew—in fact, she made her own patterns and sewed many of the clothes my sisters and I wore to school.

Dad was a lifelong motorcyclist, and safety had always been important to him. The leather gear that some of the larger riders wore never fit his long arms and slender build. It was no surprise after my Mom bought an industrial sewing machine that she was able to customize a pattern and make my Dad his first leather jacket and pants. That is how their business was born, and it became successful through word of mouth, with little to no advertising. Their customers grew to include not only motorcycle enthusiasts but anyone wanting a custom-made leather garment.

I consider myself pretty lucky to have seen a good portion of the United States from the back of Dad's motorcycle. The memories flood in. I pull on my helmet, zip up my leather jacket and throw my leg over the seat. I lean into the wind and allow it to soothe me. The engine hums as we ride through the majestic countryside. I love the sound of the tires as they roll along the pavement. No cares or worries as I rest my hands on top of my legs and I am seated right in back of him. Just the two of us on this big motorcycle, I feel the wind on my face and I am *free*. We peacefully travel along new roads and experience an unobstructed view of the landscape and I feel safe here, on this bike and in his presence.

I spent my summers touring, working and learning. My family traveled across the country and set up our custom-made leather booth at a variety of trade shows, and it was through those experiences that I learned a great deal about people and business.

I wanted Dad to know how grateful I was for the impactful experience he and Mom offered me as an impressionable young girl. During my next visit with my dad, our conversation took on a melancholy, nostalgic theme, so I shared my feelings about the family business.

Dad added that he and my mom often wondered if they made the right decisions when it came to involving us three girls in the family business.

Those comments surprised me because, from my perspective, my parents seemed quite confident in their parenting, so I never thought they had reservations about their choices, especially concerning the family business.

The following Monday morning felt mundane as I stood gazing into my jewelry box. I used my index finger to numbingly move the pieces around that had piled up on top of each other as I attempted to find a hidden treasure to compliment my work outfit.

As I stood with the lid of my jewelry box open, I thought about the importance jewelry holds for me, especially the jewelry that used to be worn by special people in my life. Their jewelry, their possessions, make me feel a certain closeness to them.

On this particular Monday morning, I chose a necklace that belonged to my mother-in-law, Laverne, or Mom Abels. The heart-shaped locket adorned with a red gemstone had tarnished over the years, adding to its authentic vintage look. I chose it because I wanted something that once rested against her heart to rest against my heart. Over the years my jewelry box has safely secured many sentimental gifts.

Some of my treasured pieces include a ring that my paternal grandpa made, a ring from my paternal great-grandmother and earrings from my mother-in-law.

As I chose jewelry on that Monday morning, I realized I had nothing that belonged to my mother. I thought about asking my dad if I could have a piece of her jewelry. My mom never wore anything fancy or pricey, and the only piece of jewelry she wore consistently was her white gold wedding band. She never pierced her ears, but years ago I recalled her wearing some of the screw-on type earrings that belonged to my paternal grandma. When she worked outside of the home, and on special occasions, she wore costume jewelry. I thought about it for a while and believed my dad would be okay with my special request. In fact, I thought, perhaps he would be pleased that I wanted to have something of hers.

I called my dad, and we agreed on a convenient time for me to come for a visit. When I arrived, we made the usual small talk and caught up a bit. I felt comfortable, and I thought it would be a good time to ask for the favor.

"I don't know if you've given any of Mom's belongings to my sisters or your granddaughters, but I was wondering if I might be able to have something of Mom's, perhaps a piece of jewelry?"

My dad stared at the floor and was silent. I felt that I had broached a sensitive subject that made him uncomfortable. A part of me wanted to back off, but the other part of me felt pretty determined, so I pressed on.

"Dad, it doesn't have to be anything special. I just thought if I could look through some of her costume jewelry, maybe there would be something that would call my name."

I felt awkward as I sat in a silent room. I asked for something that had put my dad in some sort of trance. Without making eye contact with me, he responded, "Well, sure."

He got up and walked to the dining room table. He pointed toward a crystal necklace that was hanging from the light fixture above the table. It didn't look familiar and seemed to be more expensive than the jewelry I was used to seeing my mom wear. I reminded my dad that I was more interested in something that held sentimental value for me, perhaps something I remembered her wearing. Feeling discouraged, as if I had asked for something I didn't deserve, I realized this whole thing had not turned out how I had hoped. He walked out of the dining room, toward the master bedroom (which I don't think had been used since my mom died), and I followed as he passed through the doorway.

Still in a trance-like state, he pointed at the bathroom counter and said, "There might be something in here that you would like."

The master bath is a grand room, and I was reminded of how excited my mom was to have such a luxurious and spacious bathroom. It had a walk-in closet, a soaking tub, and a double vanity. The sinks were separated by a makeup mirror complete with a white, leather cushioned chair, where she sat and got presentable for the day. I believed the master bathroom was one of her favorite rooms in their house. My dad pointed at what appeared to be some sort of jewelry holder. It was made out of wood and had, from what I could tell, a T-shaped post attached to the center, where necklaces hung. In my head, I replayed a scene from *Christmas Vacation*, where the son is handed a huge ball of tangled outdoor Christmas lights and is told, "Start with these."

He continued, "Your niece likes to play with some of Mom's necklaces. Maybe there would be something in here that you would like to have." (The niece I've never met. She was born after our family fall-out)

From a tangled mess of necklaces, he pulled one apart from the others to show me.

"How 'bout this one?"

I replied, "I don't remember that one."

We spent several minutes trying to untangle what had become my niece's toy collection. It was painful to watch my dad sort through the mess. I felt bad for asking, but I also felt deserving. I tried to help as he bumbled around clumsily, trying to free one stupid piece of cheap jewelry from the other. I became both embarrassed and pissed at the same time. *For Christ's sake, Dad, she's my mom, and I have nothing of hers. Do you think you could spare one fucking piece of crap jewelry?*

To end the misery for both of us, I chose a necklace that had somehow freed itself from the mess.

Done.

Over.

Jesus that sucked!

I held up the necklace, and with a respectful tone, I said, "Thank you, Dad. I appreciate having this, it truly means a lot."

At that point, all I wanted to do was leave. I felt my dad would have liked for me to leave as well. I was ready to leave, but instead my dad's hand landed on my shoulder as he guided me toward my mom's closet. He opened the 1980s mirrored closet doors, and a wave of deep sorrow washed over me. My assumptions were extinguished and tears welled up as I stood in my mom's closet. I assumed that my dad had given all of my mom's things to my sisters and my nieces. I remembered thinking about being left out of that ceremonial, heart-wrenching event. I envisioned my sisters sharing sweet stories as they sorted and folded, deciding who would get what. I remembered making myself feel better by believing there was nothing I wanted.

I heard my tear hit the carpet in a quiet thud, bringing me back to my dad's voice. All of her clothes were hanging in the closet. Her shoes were neatly paired on the floor beneath her clothes. Her purses and other accessories were arranged on the shelves above the clothes. My dad started to move the hangers along the clothes rod and gently ran his hand down the side of each piece of clothing as he looked at it. He asked, "Would you like some of Mom's clothes?"

He told me about each garment and where she wore it and how much she liked it. I answered softly, "No, that's okay, Dad, I don't need any of Mom's clothes."

He responded by acknowledging that my mom was a lot larger than I was, but continued to look through the assortment of her garments. He then turned his attention to the shoes and accessories. My thoughts began to drift, and I no longer had any idea what he was saying. It had become obvious that it was too painful for my dad to part with any of my mom's belongings and that that was why he couldn't part with a piece of her jewelry either.

When my mom died, I was swimming in a pool of misery, betrayal, and anger. As I stood in my mom's closet, I was glad, in a way, that my dad hadn't gone through any of her things. Sad but glad. Perhaps his plan included the inevitable future of his passing, and he figured his three daughters could go through all of their belongings at the same time. Perhaps, he thought, by then we would all be getting along.

As the visit continued to grow more uncomfortable, I became very quiet as I witnessed the truth of how much pain and deep denial my dad was in. I felt guilty that I had asked for something he was not ready to relinquish. He brought me back into the master bedroom and started pointing to the pictures on the wall, which were mostly of me and my sisters growing up. He looked at each one and reminisced. I obediently followed as he moved into the hallway off of the kitchen, where there were more pictures hung on the wall. Wedding photos of his three girls with their *big and uglies,* (my dad referred to Russ and my sister's husbands as big and uglies). *Well, he didn't smash the picture of Russ and me, so I guess he doesn't hate us.* There were more pictures of grandchildren, the ones he spends time with and the ones he doesn't. I listened to his heartfelt thoughts and followed as he led me through his gallery.

Confused, I felt as if I had forced my dad to deal with something he was not ready to face, yet he invited me into the Mom shrine and asked me to stroll down memory lane with him. When we were done looking at the photo gallery that hung on all the walls of my parents' home, I thanked my dad again for the necklace and explained that it meant a great deal to me to be able to wear it. I gave him a kiss goodbye, told him I loved him, and headed home.

I often wear the necklace my dad gave me when I want to feel my mom next to my heart. I must confess, sometimes I think more about the way it was acquired and the events around that awkward afternoon than the necklace itself. Nothing has changed at my dad's house. My mother's clothes will continue to collect dust until one of us girls or all of us are forced to determine their fate. I understand that my dad won't—and more importantly, can't—get rid of them. I witnessed my dad's deep sorrow and grief for the first time on what I will always refer to as *necklace day* at his house. Dad exposed the loneliness that lives in his heart. I recognized a familiar pattern but also experienced a side of my dad I seldom was allowed to see. He allowed the rose-colored glasses to come off for a short time and invited me through his house and explained how important *The Things* were . . . exactly where they were the day my mom died and where they will remain until he's gone.

The following morning while on my way to work, I passed the house next door to my dad's place, and my attention settled on the blue pickup truck that had been parked and unmoved for several years. I thought about the loss the family had to endure, and I wondered why they never moved the truck or sold it. The blue truck family's children are older than my children; their kids were teenagers when my kids were in grade school. They seemed very nice, *as if that had anything to do with their tragedy.* This family suffered the loss of their son at his own hand. I remembered my mom cried when she told me she heard that young man's poor mother scream when she found him. The blue truck belonged to their beloved son. Perhaps it had been too difficult to part with. Perhaps it was and continues to be a sublime reminder for them. There may be all sorts of reasons, and I don't know what they were, but it brought me to my next thought. As I drove past their house and looked at their boy's blue truck, I thought, *there is no grief clock. Grief is a private practice.* It is not up to me to determine how or for how long anyone grieves.

Teaching Moment: We should not pass judgment on anyone for any reason. I feel strongly about this statement, including how someone grieves. Some may believe it's better to get rid of everything right away and move on. Others may argue that it is too painful to get rid of objects that belonged to their loved ones. As I drove by the blue truck house and my dad's house, I realized it was not up to me, or anyone else, in what way or for how long my dad grieves. I was shocked to see all of my mother's belongings just as they were the day she left for her first and last leukemia treatment. If she were to walk back into this life, everything would be waiting for her just as she had left it. I can't imagine losing a child, and I understand holding on to objects—after all, it was the very reason I asked my dad for a piece of my mom's jewelry. For me, it's a memory, a feeling, a connection to that person through an object. The blue truck was a powerful image for me, and it offered me peace and perspective about yesterday's interaction with my dad.

MY SOUL CONTRACT

Chapter 12

Permission and Loss

In April 2001, when my father-in-law was put into hospice care, the personnel explained the measures they would take to keep my father-in-law comfortable. They gave us literature to read to educate and prepare us for his end of life journey. Russ and I read the literature while hospice set up Dad A's room.

When we were told we could go in the last room he would have at the hospital, my father-in-law was alert and was the same Larry I had always known. Nothing seemed different except for the fact that we all understood that we would say our final goodbyes in that room. Russ was strong, I was not. Russ and his dad talked business first. Pop, as Russ lovingly called his dad, had raised his son to know when the time came there would be exact steps to follow concerning his affairs. Dad Abels went through his mental list as Russ nodded in agreement. I was impressed by what they had discussed. It was a quiet interaction, and there was nothing left to question regarding his wishes.

It felt right and important for Russ and me to give Nick and Derrick (aged nine and ten) an opportunity to say goodbye to their grandpa. Witnessing our boys say goodbye to one of their favorite people in their world was one of the most heart-wrenching moments of our lives. It was important and delicate and sweet, and by far one of the most difficult things I've ever had to watch.

I was amazed at how all of the things that seemed important the day before were no longer important. Every problem felt miniscule. Nothing felt real. Work didn't matter. Eating and sleeping didn't matter. The only thing that mattered was the love in that room and spending time together. I began to question why I had put so much emphasis on things that suddenly felt so unimportant.

The doctors made it sound like my father-in-law wouldn't make it more than a day or two, but to our surprise, it turned out to be several days. I remembered thinking, *Typical Pop, stubborn and bullheaded. He will decide when it's time to go, not the doctors.*

After a few days and according to the pamphlets the hospice nurses gave Russ and me to read, Dad A's body was showing signs of dying. I held his hand and told my dear, sweet father-in-law that we would understand if he needed to go. I leaned in close and whispered in his ear, "You fought a good fight, and we will miss you so much. We will all be okay."

I continued, "Mom is waiting for you. It's okay if you need to go."

He hadn't made too much noise up to that point, but when I mentioned my mother-in-law, he grunted at me. I wondered if I upset him by saying what I had. I hoped not. I wanted to share what I believed, and I believed she was there. I thought and hoped that the grunt was an acknowledgment that he had heard me and he could see the love of his life waiting for him.

My sister-in-law flew in from New York when she heard the news about her dad, and never left his side. Russ had convinced her to leave the hospital for a while and come back to our house to get showered and eat and perhaps sleep in a real bed for one night. She agreed and had no sooner walked in our house when the hospital called with the sad news.

Pop set his own rules just as he had his whole life. His death was on his terms, and he wanted to be alone, perhaps to spare his children that memory. I admire and respect how he chose to take his last breath.

Nine years later, after I said what I needed to say to my mother, I gave her the same permission. Perhaps the permission was more for me so I could let her go. My mom chose to have her family around her bedside to witness her last breath. Even though our family was broken, her departure was about love and togetherness, and that is how she wanted it.

There are different degrees of loss. I believe that when we witness someone or something die, it changes us forever.

Chapter 13

The Power of Spirit

I met Karen at my new place of employment in March 2006, where I had accepted the position as the accounts payable administrator. Upon meeting her, I felt drawn to her kind and gentle spirit. I witnessed her warm interactions with other employees and enjoyed her good sense of humor and quick wit. Karen was fun and smart and loyal, and although I didn't even know what it meant at the time, we were kindred spirits.

After a few months, I had developed friendships with a few of the office girls. We made it a point to get together outside of work, which provided an opportunity for me to get to know each of them better. We always laughed and had a good time, but some of my favorite times were spent discussing deep, introspective topics. It was during these personal conversations that I learned more about Karen. She was aware and conscious. She possessed spiritual wisdom and was willing to share her insights with me. As our friendship grew, she provided a safe space for me to share my experiences. In 2006, I learned why she was put on my path. Karen was one of my spiritual teachers.

I used to not question or investigate anything. I was naïve and trusting. I believed what I was told was the truth because *I* told the truth. I believed people had my best interest at heart because *I* had their best interest at heart. I believed people had good intentions because *I* had good intentions. To me, every attribute, every speck of a person's character sat directly on the surface. There was no need to dig any further than what I saw right in front of me. I was comfortable believing that everyone was who they projected themselves to be. I lacked confidence and the skills to investigate or ask about anything that lived beyond the surface. I spared myself and anyone I knew any uncomfortable feelings surrounding deeper, more personal queries. I did not possess an internal nudge to know more. I had no interest in understanding why something happened or why a person was the way they were.

I didn't question my mother or my father. When I would ask, "Why?" they would answer, "Because I said so."

I didn't experience a great deal of explaining, so when "Because I said so" was the answer and because I was an obedient daughter, I learned not to pursue my inquiries any further. Perhaps my parents didn't know the answers to my questions. Or maybe they were repeating the behaviors their parents had taught them. Maybe they were bored and tired. In any event, I didn't want to be a bother, and I learned to accept their answers as gospel.

One day, Karen and I were sharing stories about peculiar things that we had experienced surrounding the topic of ghosts and spirits. We shared our personal beliefs about spirits and whether or not our dearly departed had the ability to visit us. More specifically, we discussed ways in which spirits could communicate with us. Karen explained that oftentimes, we may feel a connection with a specific sign or a symbol that represents the spirit of a loved one.

Karen shared an exercise that she and her sister had heard about and tried. The spiritual experiment involved choosing an object to represent a deceased loved one. The object should be identifiable and have significant meaning for you. The object chosen would then be the symbol you ask a specific spirit to send to you.

I was eager try the exercise. I took some time to choose meaningful objects for each of the three important spirits of significant people I anticipated connecting with.

The first spirit I wanted to communicate with was my mother. The symbol I chose for her was a black rose. The black rose I pictured was from my mother's simple yet elegant china pattern. I had been enamored with my mother's china set since I was a little girl. It was the one object I thought about inheriting when she died. The pattern seemed out of time or perhaps ahead of its time. I had never seen anything like it before. Most china patterns I was familiar with had petite, pastel-colored flowers of pinks, yellows, and blues. Mom's pattern was a single, delicate, black rose bud with its prickly green stem, which hugged the curve of the pewter-trimmed alabaster plate.

The second spirit I wanted to communicate with was Dad Abels. I chose a tea set as my symbol for him. One evening, soon after Mom Abels passed away, Russ and I had stopped over to visit my father-in-law. As I entered the kitchen, I noticed the tea set right away. He had it displayed on the sill of the counter that separated the kitchen from the dining room. I recalled seeing it at some point during our many years in their home, but it had never been presented in that particular spot. It was so pretty, and I commented on how much I liked it. As I walked closer to admire the charming set, he said, "I'm glad you like it, Mic, cuz I'd like for you to have it."

I was overcome by his kind gesture. It was such a thoughtful and unexpected gift. The tea set is proudly displayed in my home. It has been kept safe in a curio cabinet, and I am reminded often of its significance.

The third spirit I wanted to communicate with was my sweet mother-in-law. I chose a brown couch to symbolize Mom Abels. I reminisced about our relationship and the many conversations that drew us closer when we used to sit next to each other on that brown couch. I was able to talk to Mom Abels about things I couldn't discuss with my own mother. She was patient and kind and offered wisdom that lived within her friendship. She listened with her eyes and held me in her heart. In my opinion, she was the definition of a lady. I never heard her speak ill of anyone or hold judgment. She was supportive and loving and strong. Mom Abels told me things that I felt were in confidence. She invited me into her private world as she shared her personal stories and life experiences. I kept them safe in my heart to recall when I needed to remember her grace. I felt a special closeness and loyalty to her. She was one of the warmest, sweetest people I have had the pleasure of knowing in my lifetime.

At least a month had passed before I noticed any proof of communication with the spirits of my loved ones. When I realized they were communicating with me, I learned that the character of the person who had crossed over was a mirror image of the spirit's personality. I also learned not to expect the symbol that I chose to appear how I pictured it.

It was December, and Russ and I had a meeting with Marsha, our trusted loan officers, at the local bank. During our appointment, I noticed a rose-shaped ring on Marsha's finger. It was so delicate and reminded me of a soapstone ring I had seen years earlier. *Hmmm. It was a rose, but it was off-white, not black. Not my sign.* The ring got my attention, so much so that I had a difficult time paying attention to our conversation. My thoughts drifted as I looked around Marsha's office, pretending to pay attention to the conversation. I noticed some pictures on Marsha's desk, and there was one in particular that piqued my interest. When we were finished discussing business, I pointed at the picture of the little girl and asked Marsha who she was. Marsha's face lit up, and she smiled as she stated that the picture was of her granddaughter. She explained that her young granddaughter had suffered a hearing loss. I, too, had suffered a hearing loss as a child. Intrigued, I asked several questions and listened as Marsha shared the experiences they had been through because of the hearing loss. Our meeting ended but before pushing my chair in, I asked one last question. "What is your granddaughter's name?"

Marsha grinned at the photograph and answered, "Rose."

Hmmm, was this my black rose symbol? Was my mom being her typical clever self? After all, Marsha and her granddaughter are African American. I was very curious but not thoroughly convinced.

The following day was Sunday, and it was bitterly cold. Russ started a fire in the woodburning stove, and we decided to watch a movie while I paid some bills and enjoyed a lazy Sunday. About thirty minutes into the movie, Russ got up to let our dog, Izzy, out and have a smoke. One of the actors in the movie was Samuel L.

Jackson. I didn't recognize the young actress playing his daughter, but her character's name was Rose. *Another black rose? Two days in a row.* It seemed coincidental to say the least. I listened to the dialogue but took my eyes off of the television screen to write a check to the gas company. Then I heard my mother's first and last name in a man's voice coming from the TV. Startled and confused, my attention shot back to the television screen because I couldn't believe what I had just heard. We didn't have a recording device at the time or any way of rewinding the movie back to verify what I had just heard. Russ was still outside with Izzy, so I could not ask him. I sat in sheer awe and disbelief.

Glancing up at the ceiling, I thought, *Mom, did you just communicate with me?* I realized the moment was intended only for me. I couldn't tell Russ; he would have thought I was nuts. Allowing my thoughts to return to yesterday's visit with Marsha, I realized my mom's first attempt to connect was not enough for me to believe. The second black Rose got my attention, but I questioned it as a strange coincidence. But when I heard a man's voice say my mother's full name over the television speakers, in a movie with a black girl named Rose that convinced me that my mother's spirit was communicating with me.

The second confirmation came from Dad Abels. I used to say that I don't dream, but the experts say we dream every night. It had been a very long time, years in fact, since I had remembered a dream. But I won't ever forget this one.

Dad Abels had a great sense of humor, and he enjoyed making people laugh. He was also a bit of a prankster. He loved to tease people and play tricks on them, particularly me. I was an easy target. As a sensitive sixteen-year-old when I met Russ's dad, I remembered one night Russ had to ask his dad to lighten up a little with the teasing because I was so sensitive about it.

Dad Abels loved the game of golf and was an avid player. He enjoyed most of his retirement on the links near his home.

The dream played like a movie. I saw my father-in-law's face, big as life, right in front of me, and he was laughing. The laugh started as a chuckle and developed into a hysterical belly laugh. Dad Abels laughed and threw his head back like he had just gotten me with one of his one-liners. I got the distinct impression he was quite pleased with himself.

In my peripheral vision, multicolored golf tees began to appear. They moved in choreographed animation as if they were dancing. I watched as each golf tee danced in front of me. They danced and my father-in-law laughed. That was the extent of my dream.

I was anxious to share the details of my dream with Karen. The dreams Karen had and described to me were extremely vivid and colorfully detailed, and since we enjoyed attempting to interpret the meanings of each one, I looked forward to hearing her interpretation of mine. I felt as though I had crossed the threshold of dream accomplishments because I not only remembered my dream but I dreamt in color.

"I had a crazy dream last night, can I tell you about it?"

Karen responded, "Absolutely."

"Well, the dream was just my father-in-law laughing hysterically, with a bunch of golf tees dancing around. His face disappeared, but I could still hear him laughing like he had just told a really good joke."

Karen listened and said, "That's weird."

"Yeah, and what's with the set of tees?"

As soon as I said the words *set of tees*, it hit me. I stopped myself and said, "Oh my goodness, Karen, it's a tee set! It's not *the* tea set, but it's a tee set, and that's the symbol I asked for."

Ecstatic with my discovery, I continued, "It would be just like him to trick me and laugh, saying, you want a tea set? I'll give you a tee set!"

I sent a silent message to my father-in-law. *Thank you, Dad. You were listening, and you came through loud and clear.*

The brown couch, the symbol for Mom Abels, took a bit longer to show up. I believe she kept trying, but I was skeptical of anything that was not definitively the actual sign. There was a fresh blanket of snow covering the ground when I got up in the middle of the night to get a drink of water. As I walked down the hall toward the living room, there was a bright light shining on my husband's recliner. It reminded me of when the moon is bright and the light reflects off of the snow. The light had somehow ricocheted onto the chair, but when I walked over to the chair and looked out the window it was very cloudy and I couldn't see the moon. When I looked back at the chair, the light was gone. I got my drink of water and went back to bed. I pulled the covers up to my chin and thought about Mom Abels. The light on the brown chair made me think of her. I wrestled with the fact that I had specifically asked for a couch, not a chair.

A couple of nights later I was driving home from work. The rural roads I travel to get home are paved but not well lit and not cleared well during snow season. There's a one-mile stretch in particular that's very dark because there're no streetlamps and very few houses. My night vision is not that of a twenty-five-year-old anymore, so I tend to drive a bit slower at night. Along this one-mile stretch, there were four or five houses all on the west side of the street. The east side is all farm fields, so I always pay close attention for any critters that may dart out onto my path. It was after 5 p.m. and it was pitch-black. I didn't see anything until I was almost right in front of it. At the last minute, I swerved. My heart was racing, and I was shocked and scared as I tried to figure out what the hell was on the road. It was huge. I looked in my rearview mirror, but the road was so dark I couldn't see what I had avoided. I was worried that the next motorist wouldn't be so lucky. The roads were icy and snow-packed, and I decided I would cause more danger for myself and others if I backtracked to investigate. I don't know what I would have done anyway. Whatever that thing was, it was too big to move by myself. I was sure it was an object, not an animal. I got home safely, prepared dinner, and went to bed. It was my typical evening routine, and I didn't think any more about the incident on the road.

The next morning, on my way to work, I drove my usual route and was on the same road where I almost hit the mystery object the night before. I slowed down when I came close to where I believed the incident had happened, and then I saw it. There, on the side of the road, was a big brown couch! I laughed out loud and exclaimed, "No shit!"

It was clear to me at that moment that I needed big stuff for spirit to get my attention.

Teaching Moment: I am a believer. They are here. Our dead people are here. Their spirits are able to communicate with us. Ask for signs. Be open to receive. Observe and pay attention, or just have the TV talk directly to you, or have a huge couch jump out in front of your car. I think I can still hear Dad Abels laughing. I think they are all laughing!

While sitting quietly, with the intention to open communication with your loved one, bring into your mind's eye the image of your loved one and the image of your symbol. With an open heart, release the image of your symbol along with your intention to communicate with your loved one into the universe. Ask your loved one to bring that sign or symbol to you. When you see the symbol, it confirms that your loved one's spirit received your message and acknowledged your request. The exercise will confirm that you have connected on a spiritual level with your dearly departed.

Chapter 14

Numbers, Ghosts, and Spirits

Tiny eyes acknowledge the familiar. Simultaneously their gaze is pulled over my left shoulder as we experience the divine existence of a weightless, floating mist as it presents itself freely. Harmoniously. Lovingly. As I bathe my babies too young to be left alone, I am drawn to search out our mystery guest. Slowly I rise, keeping one eye on my boys and one on the corridor. As I round the corner where the unknown was headed, all I see is darkness. Nothingness. Vanished.

I have always referred to myself as a numbers girl. I have been involved in accounting since I entered the workforce, beginning in my parents' shop. My mom taught me bookkeeping, learning at an early age about debits and credits, accounts payable, and accounts receivable. I learned how to track overhead expenses and figure payroll and payroll taxes. I took care of invoices, receipts, and billing.

When I learned, back in the late 1970s, all record keeping was done by hand, in pencil on ledger paper.

My obsession with numbers made it easy for me to remember birthdays, addresses, license plate numbers, and phone numbers. I believe that's a left-brain thing. Analytical vs. creative. I excelled in math all through school, and I used my math skills to place myself in a comfortable little box that has kept me in accounting. I did not go to college after high school. I worked as a bank teller after graduation and stayed until December 1992, when Derrick was born. Russ and I decided it was more important for me to stay home and raise our boys than to work and pay a day care provider most of my salary. I welcomed my full-time mom role and passionately engaged in all of the experiences that developed from the special time I was able to spend with my boys. When Nick and Derrick were both in school, I decided to enter the workforce again, and it was in accounting.

In 2012, numbers began to have a different meaning for me. I started to notice repetitive numbers. I started seeing the number one repeated. Throughout the day, when I'd look at a digital clock it would read 11:11 or 1:11. I began seeing the number one repetitively show up on my receipts at work too. Soon, I began to see other numbers appear in repetitive form: 222, 333, 444, 555, and so on. It was happening often enough that it felt strange. The occurrence went beyond a shoulder shrug or a curious coincidence. I went to my friend Karen for answers, support, and guidance. When I told Karen about the numbers I had been seeing, she explained that seeing the number one repeatedly is a spiritual gift and that angels send numbers to get our attention.

I had experienced seeing repetitive numbers at home and at work for a few weeks when I witnessed a strange coincidence at work. I was seated at my desk in a high-back office chair when I felt someone come up behind me and grab the back of the chair and give it a yank. I smiled and quickly turned around, expecting to catch the prankster. To my surprise, there was nobody standing there. I thought that was odd because, there was nobody fast enough to make it out of my cubicle and down the hallway without me hearing or seeing them. On three consecutive days, the same yanking of my chair happened, and the repetitive occurrence felt strange. I felt like a kid that got picked on. I decided to ask the person in the office who was basically a grown-up adolescent—the guy who acts like he's in junior high—if he had been messing with my chair. I could tell by the look on his face that he had no idea what I was talking about.

The following Saturday, a brilliantly gorgeous July afternoon, I attended a friend's wedding. The bride, my sweet friend April, chose a wedding venue that made it difficult for me to decide whether or not I could attend. Upon receiving the wedding invitation, I learned that it was to be held at my sister and brother-in-law's business. I was torn between attending my friend's wedding with the gut-wrenching possibility of seeing my sister after all these years and not attending the wedding, with the risk of hurting my friend. I decided it was best to tell my friend the truth about my family fallout. I explained that I had good intentions of wanting to see her get married, but if it became too uncomfortable for me, I might have to leave. April understood, and although it felt awkward to share my story, the situation called for my truth. I knew Russ would not be able to attend, but Karen and some other people I knew would be there as well.

Seeing my sister at my friend's wedding was awkward. As my sister was working, I passed her and held out my hand to touch her arm and said, "Hi."

That simple gesture removed all the weirdness from the evening, and I was able to be present and enjoy the wedding festivities.

Later in the evening, I joined Karen and her sister on the venue's huge wraparound porch. We were talking and laughing and enjoying the summer evening when all of a sudden I felt a familiar tug on the back of my chair. The back of the white wicker chair I was seated on was higher than my head. It was against the porch railing, and beyond the railing was a three-foot drop off that was densely planted. The landscape was gorgeous, and every inch of the ground was covered with a variety of plants, bushes, and flowers. As soon as I felt the tug at the back of my chair, I turned around, only to find nobody there. I looked at Karen and asked, "Did you see what just happened?"

Cocking her head to the side, Karen responded, "Did I see what?"

Dumbfounded, I asked, "Was someone standing behind me just now?"

Karen laughed. "No, nobody was near you."

Since I had shared my work chair story with Karen, I explained that the same thing had just happened. Karen confirmed again that no one was behind me or on the side of me or anywhere around me.

Why was the chair-tugging spirit here too?

The following Monday morning after the wedding, I was at work, entering data into my computer. My electric calculator was located just to the right of my keyboard. While I was typing on my computer's keyboard, the tape on my electric calculator started advancing all by itself. I looked over and couldn't believe what I was seeing. I started to hit the keys on the calculator, but the calculator wouldn't stop, and the tape continued to come out all by itself. It didn't matter how many buttons I pushed, the calculator kept running. I stood up and backed away from my desk, and the calculator finally stopped on its own. I shared the bizarre event with my coworkers.

The following day, my work calculator started to run all by itself again, just as it had the day before. I stood up and backed away from my desk, with my hands in the air. I called my coworkers over so they could witness what was happening with their own eyes. They couldn't believe what they were seeing. We all stood back and watched the calculator tape advance with nothing printed on it. Each coworker stepped closer to investigate the strange phenomenon. Just as it had the day before, the calculator stopped all by itself.

These strange events reminded me that it was not the first time I had experienced bizarre happenings. I have always been open-minded concerning ghosts or spirits, but I had a very narrow understanding of certain things in the ghost and spirit world. The events never scared me; I was intrigued and found these bizarre occurrences quite interesting.

One of these incidents happened at the store my husband and I owned and operated. Each morning when I arrived to open the store, I walked down the bread aisle and found a puddle of water in the middle of the floor. The puddle was in the same spot every single morning, without fail. There were no sources of water near the puddle that would explain how it had gotten there. The girl I opened with each morning had some ghost stories of her own. She typically arrived about an hour before me each morning but said she never saw the puddle of water. Instead, every morning she arrived at the store, a loaf of bread was in the middle of the floor, and every single morning she would pick it up and put it back on the shelf. We laughed about those strange happenings and wondered who our ghost could be.

Another encounter I experienced with ghosts was in our first and current home. Russ and I moved into our house when Nick was twenty months old and Derrick was six months old. The first few weeks kept us very busy getting our new home in order. We settled in and began to enjoy our daily routines. In a very short time, we had fallen in love with our quiet country setting.

The boys were good nappers, and like most moms, I took full advantage of their nap time, picking up around the house, washing dishes and doing the laundry. Our washer and dryer were located downstairs in an unfinished basement. When I knew the boys were fast asleep, I would head downstairs to put in a load of laundry. The first time it happened, I ran upstairs, thinking the boys woke up from their naps way too soon. I heard footsteps and thought Nick must have been running around upstairs. I bolted up the basement steps, ready to get things back in order, but when I opened their bedroom door, both boys were sound asleep. I shrugged it off and returned to the basement to finish what I was doing. I put the clothes in the washer and poured in the detergent, and that's when I heard footsteps running upstairs again. I went upstairs only to find Nick and Derrick still sound asleep. Each time I was in the basement, I heard running footsteps upstairs. There were times when I was upstairs and I heard pipes clanging downstairs. I had decided that, with my limited understanding of ghosts, this must have been the older gentleman who lived in the house before us. I will call him Grandpa E. The sound of running didn't bother me, but I did check each time to make sure my boys weren't up from their naps. The pipe banging didn't bother me either. I would yell down and say, "Hi, Grandpa E. Yes, I hear you." I thought ghosts or spirits could only be heard, felt, or seen in the places they had lived or died.

I had another encounter when my young sons and I experienced a ghost in our hallway. It was early evening, and I was giving the boys a bath before Russ got home. I had just finished bathing Derrick and pivoted slightly left to start bathing Nick. As I turned, out of the corner of my eye I saw something pass behind me in the hall. I not only saw it but I felt it. I knew it wasn't a person, but it was definitely *something*. It was a white, billowy mist that floated toward the kids' bedroom. At the exact moment I sensed we had a visitor, Nick asked, in his sweet baby voice, "Daddy home?"

I got chills, and the hair on the back of my neck stood up. Both boys were secure in their little tub seats, but I was torn between not wanting to leave them alone and wanting to investigate what I thought I had just seen. I was curious about something I could not explain and a little scared to see it again. With my heart pounding, I got up and walked toward the boys' bedroom. I peeked around the corner, walked into the bedroom, but saw nothing. It had vanished.

Teaching Moment: The things that were happening were igniting a curiosity within me. I asked to gain a deeper understanding of the spirit world. I have always believed, on a certain level that ghosts or spirits exist. Recalling past events and experiencing new events sparked a renewed interest. I believe there is something more out there. I set an intention to learn more

about the spirit world and remain curious about my interactions

with spirits.

Part II-Trust

Chrysalis

I wave goodbye and mourn the loss of my own naïveté and the way I was before. Before I became aware. Before my eyes were open. Before I knew I had a choice. Before I met my heart and chose a road less traveled. Before I decided to let my spirit steer the course to meet my soul. Before choosing my breath over my pain.

My choice was to learn all I could about me. I wanted to spiritually dive inward and honor a hermit-like quality of my soul's sanctuary and solitude. I wanted to forget my set of memorized habitual behaviors. I wanted to allow space to adopt new practices to fuel my passions.

I've always been aware of the space between. I describe it as a magnetic pull that had been with me always and existed in the median of two parallel universes. The familiar one pulls me to a place in my three-dimensional reality and lures the comfort of conformity. The same one that listens to worn-out rules and controls me with conventional obedience. The one that keeps me separate operates from fear and limits my potential. And when the lines within the space between them are questioned and are no longer so well-defined, I am pulled toward the other one . . . the one that I was born into and that my soul promised to follow. The one that resides in spiritual dimensions and catapults me forward into the life I was meant to live. The one that supports me by honoring my individuality, operates from love and ignites unlimited potential and purpose. The one that sees me in you and you in me.

The learning feels insurmountable, but I am ready to submerge myself into the depths of my inner knowing. My connection to self is beginning.

Chapter 15

Betrayal and Reevaluation

Feeling nauseous and lost, I am bobbing along on top of the waves as I drift further and further away from land. I don't recognize this place or myself. It is all so very foreign to me. Along my voyage I recognize relatives, teachers, and friends. Each wave reveals past relationships, and I am compelled to examine the evolution and value of each one. I carefully consider the relationships that gently support me and keep me buoyant. And the ones that crash into me like a harsh imbalance. I know the ones to keep and the ones that need to lovingly float away.

Betrayal shattered the trust I had wholeheartedly gifted to others and made me forget how I was once cared for. Betrayal made me forget how my mother soothed my broken teenage heart. Betrayal made me forget how my mom and dad, my sisters and I used to laugh and have fun together. Betrayal made me forget that we once had what felt like an unbreakable bond. Betrayal sent me on a journey of reevaluating my relationships with everyone. Not just my mother and father, but also other family members, friends and coworkers . . . *everyone.* At a very deep and honest level, the shock of betrayal made me move into life. It made me realize not only what I desired but what I deserved. It offered a new space to handpick the best of the best to be in my circle, my tribe. All of this and learning to be okay with that decision became paramount for me.

I experienced a deep realization that my outside world did not match my inside world. I could no longer focus my attention on matters that did not feel authentic to my spirit. My priorities changed. My desires were different. I was different. The new me and my new environment required letting go and disinvesting my energy in relationships that no longer fed my soul.

When I began to evaluate my friendships, it was very important for me to consider how each relationship had evolved. I began to question the richness and status of each one. I asked myself these questions: *Did my involvement in this relationship fill my heart, or did my heart feel empty, or worse yet, did my heart feel*

nothing? When I was in the presence of the relationship, did I feel

lighter or heavier? When we spent time together, did I feel engaged

or exhausted?

Surrounding myself with like-minded individuals was paramount for my new existence. I had to ask if my current relationships could survive in my new environment with the new me. I believe we are all students and we are all teachers. Each interaction, no matter the length of time, served a meaningful purpose in my life.

As I made the conscious decision to close my relationships with certain individuals, I held a private, silent ceremony and thanked each one for being an important part of my life. I acknowledged that they provided a true reflection of what and who I needed in my life during the time we had spent together. I thanked each person for helping me to see my sparkly warrior parts and my not-so-sparkly warrior parts. I put my hands together in prayer at the center of my heart and sent gratitude for the relationship and everything their friendship taught me. Then I bid the friendship a loving and honorable farewell.

In the early part of my spiritual awareness, I experienced an internal conflict. I had never put myself or my needs ahead of others. Although I knew how important self-awareness was for my spiritual growth, my internal dialogue told me I was being selfish and egotistical, conceited and self-centered. These were comments I grew up hearing. Labels I had been taught to identify with that were created in my external world. I lacked confidence and I put other's needs and wants ahead of my own. I said yes more than I said no. The changes I made, although deliberately guided, went against the grain of everything I grew up believing. At the same time, the changes felt invigorating. I had made myself a promise to invest in my spiritual growth, and that meant that I would need to let those old thoughts go. Letting go allowed me to introduce a future that felt fresh, free, new, and real.

I gave myself permission to emerge out of old friendships and to grow and morph into a new life that was calling me. A light was shining where it was dark, and I realized the potential of who I was supposed to be. I wanted to surround myself with the bravest and best because they are who I looked up to. They are heroes and teachers who inspire me daily. They put a smile on my face and joy in my heart.

I believe all relationships are sacred contracts. The perfect people are placed on our path at the perfect time to offer opportunities to learn our life's lessons. Each contract has different verbiage, and each contract has agreements and arrangements that may need to change or end. I have old and lasting friendships that continue to light me up, and the magical bonds within those friendships will forever be held true and dear to me. Friendships should hold joy and peace, support and love. An equal give and take to create an exquisite balance as we walk through this life together. Anything or anyone vibrating at the same frequency or at a higher frequency increases the potential for spiritual growth.

For generations, we have struggled to gain approval from our external environment. We intrinsically need it, we crave it, and it offers us an avenue for acceptance. I thought about the last conversation I had had with my mom and how I explained that although getting her approval was welcome, I didn't need it to survive. These words are tough as I think back through the entire conversation. I wanted my mom to know that I was a grown woman and capable of making big decisions concerning the well-being of my husband and my sons, personal decisions that didn't need her stamp of approval. I had never spoken to my mom like that before and I believe those words carried the sharpness that cut into her heart so deeply. I believe what my mother heard was, I don't need you.

Even though I felt very confident at the time, and I was exploring uncharted territory with my mother, I felt a role reversal, validating what the tarot card reader had told me. I felt I was the adult, and my mother, the child. It was strange but I think it explained a lot for me as I recalled carving out a dependent representation for myself to my mom. There was a definite shift that took place toward the end of that conversation. I felt bad that what I had shared was painful for her to hear, but I also felt justified as I shared what had been so important for me for so long.

Teaching Moment: I think the people in our lives are like pens or pencils. Pens are durable, committed, permanent, and stable. Pencils are indefinite, temporary, and hold a short commitment. Our connections to people can be pens or pencils. Some are here for us permanently during our entire existence, and some are temporary, only here for a brief visit. All are important and vital and teach us what we need during their collaboration in our lives. Each interaction, each experience is unique to our personal growth.

Chapter 16

Winter Trees

Winter trees stripped bare, branches spread wide open, reaching defenseless toward the sky, yet securely connected to Mother Earth. Vulnerable. Asking. Begging. Inviting the harshness of all conditions. The tree is ready, for just beneath the soil lies miles of growth, firmly rooted so as to not disturb the birthed-in spiritually supported foundation.

Once I decided it was okay and healthy for me to let go of relationships that no longer vibrated on the same frequency as the new me, it was as if the Universe offered the perfect stage to justify and support my choices. I embraced a new confidence that allowed me to tell someone that how I had been treated was unacceptable. I was able to explain the things I was no longer willing to tolerate, in a respectful manner.

In March 2006, when I landed a job in the accounting office, I was expected to dress in business attire every day. The office atmosphere felt fancy and I was anxious to embrace my new role and dress up every day. I rewarded myself with a set of sculptured nails. Perfect nails to match my perfect outfits in my perfect, new office in a perfect environment. I found a salon conveniently located near my new place of employment, with a manicurist who was perfect for me. Since I would be going to my appointments every three weeks, distance was important in making my salon selection.

In December 2011, after having acrylic nails for five years, I wrestled with the idea of giving them up based on my new ideals. The nails were fake. I had been making changes to support a more natural approach to what I put in my body, so I started to make changes that affected the outside of my body .

The event for me was symbolic and fed my inner warrior. Something I was not used to doing unless it was fueled by intense pain or anger.

I was five minutes late for my nail appointment, and the manicurist called my cell phone twice as I made my way across town. While stopping at the traffic light, I listened to her message and felt she was being a bit over-concerned. When I arrived at the salon, I sat down across from her and made the necessary apologies.

I had three broken nails, which meant she would need a bit more time. She expressed to me that she wished I would have let her know so she could have scheduled accordingly. I had had broken nails at other appointments with her, and she had never expressed that it was a problem before.

She was not her usual chatty self and appeared to be distracted. While she worked, I attempted to make small talk. I noticed she was interested in the time and kept looking at her phone. She placed the nail forms on my broken nails and worked quickly. As she used the acrylic powder to build my new nails, I sensed her frustration was also building. I stopped making small talk, and the silence must have made her uncomfortable. She explained that one of her difficult clients was scheduled for right after me and she would become very upset if her appointment was delayed. It became obvious to me that my manicurist had a scheduling issue. In the past, she had shared stories about this particular client and how she had caused her so much grief.

Her anxiety increased and she was no longer mindful of my time. I had always had a good relationship with her, and I felt I was a good, reliable client. I was on time, I never canceled an appointment, and I tipped well. Her behavior had me feeling rushed and undervalued. She excused herself for a moment, and I watched as she got up to check the waiting area in the front of the salon. It was obvious to me that she was looking to see if her next client had arrived yet. While she was gone, I started writing my check for the day's services. I decided it would be my last appointment. I put my checkbook away, and when she returned she was even more distressed. Evidently, Miss Difficult Client was already waiting. The whole thing didn't make sense as I had only been in her chair for about thirty minutes. My entire appointment usually lasted over an hour. When she settled back into her chair to resume work, I pulled my hand away. I reached for my purse, removed my check for the usual amount, *without tip this time*, and I said, "You are having a hard time focusing on me right now, so I will finish these up at home." I tore my check out, handed her the Christmas gift I brought for her, and wished her happy holidays.

She pleaded with me to stay and apologized several times. I told her that she made it clear that her other client was more important, so our appointment was over. I left and headed straight for the beauty supply store. I bought acetone and files. The acetone would help lift the acrylic off my natural nails, and the files would buff what was left of my real nails. My manicurist presented me with a perfect scenario to let her go. Her actions enabled me to relinquish something I no longer needed or wanted. I had developed a friendship with her, and she shared her personal affairs with me. Part of what she had shared was her declining client list and financial hardship. Guilt kept me scheduling appointments, as I would have been partly to blame for lessening her income. The perfect scenario had been placed in front of me. It validated my choice, and I realized I was important to my manicurist, until I wasn't.

I was not valued in that situation. My intuition sent a warning signal to pay attention to the strong contradiction between the life I was pursuing and the way she treated me. I consider myself to be a highly sensitive person. I am affected by what others say and do, and I absorb their words like emotional testimony. I am learning to be unapologetic about this. Being a sensitive individual is precious and a valuable gift to possess. I knew I must learn to pay attention and take notice when inner chaos settles in and my emotional balance becomes disturbed.

Incidents like this made me realize that there were other individuals on my path who no longer fed my emotional energy. Their actions were a disruption to the values I deemed important in my life. It was time to let my fake nails go, and it was time to let my manicurist go. I was able to release the relationship with gratitude in my heart and acknowledge that I had grown because of it.

In a non-confrontational situation, I chose to let go of something that no longer nurtured me. There was no need to be hurtful. When I respected my healthy boundaries and honored my truth, I knew my decisions would be the right ones.

I wanted to be more mindful of not only how I interacted with others but how I interacted with myself. I began paying attention to the thoughts and comments that went through my mind. I was shocked to discover that most of my thoughts were negative. I noticed how reactive I was in my thoughts, and I wanted to develop a discipline to change. I would never allow a friend to speak to herself in the way I was speaking to myself. I decided that I would begin to talk to myself as I would a dear friend. I wanted to create an awareness so that I could change a defensive, negative thought or reaction to a more nurturing, caring response. I discovered the way I thought about myself and the reactions I had toward others were a direct contradiction of the way I wanted to feel in my life. The practice of paying attention was a discipline I was wholeheartedly ready to activate.

I developed a new habit. I learned to catch myself when a negative thought popped in, and I learned to change it immediately. I experienced self-limiting thoughts, and oftentimes they were directly connected to my perceptions about my body or my job performance, and sometimes it was an unnecessary comment that I wished I could take back.

"Mindful thought redirection" became the name of my newest tool in my self-help toolbox. Mindful thought redirection demands self-awareness. The following provides an example of how mindful thought redirection worked to benefit my emotional health and well-being.

I caught myself being triggered while out to dinner with a friend. My much thinner friend ordered a decadent dessert after our healthy meal. I felt unworthy of such a treat because I lacked control around food. My self-talk was beating me up. I knew my thoughts of self-judgment were based on what I believed other people might think about me. My inner dialogue was attached to my outer world. Even though I fought my whole life to keep and maintain a healthy weight, I lost the battle most of the time. In the past, it wouldn't have mattered whether I had reached a desired number on the scale or not, I habitually carried around negative thoughts about my weight.

Now, as soon as I caught my negative thoughts, I mindfully redirected my thought patterns and asked myself, *what are you afraid of?* I pictured my thoughts leaving my mind, and I guided them toward my heart. I methodically tapped into my heart and changed the chatter to reflect what love-based self-talk would sound like. *My body is beautiful and strong inside and out. It works hard to keep me healthy every day. I will continue to make choices to respect the vessel I have been gifted. I honor the choices I've made. I am healthy, strong, curvy, voluptuous, and sexy.*

I might get the dessert or I might not, but I've made the decision from a place of love, not fear. I am learning how to take cues from my heart, allowing it to pump fresh perspectives of love into my thoughts. With dedication and practice, I believed I could change my mind, literally.

Teaching Moment: While making decisions or simply beginning the exercise of paying attention to our thoughts, it is imperative to recognize that there are two emotional operating systems: fear and love. I describe it as simple as head and heart. Thoughts derived from fear are constant head chatter that never stops. The ego defends us while constantly berating us. The ego is on a mission to compare ourselves to how people act and look, to the things they own and the places they live. Ego reminds us that we are not good enough, pretty enough, skinny enough, smart enough, rich enough, or nice enough. Self-limiting thoughts support self-limiting feelings of lack and self-doubt. Fear presents itself as lack, separation, defensiveness, inadequacy, failure, judgment, anger, and losing control. Our egos respond defensively when we choose fear.

Thoughts derived from love come from your heart. We have been conditioned to pay attention to what we perceive as negative. We have not been conditioned to pay attention to ourselves and our thinking or to care about how we are thinking. Love-based thinking closes the gap of separation. Love-based thinking includes acts of kindness, care, compassion, gratitude, empathy, connection, peace, and joy. The act of listening to your heart will enrich and broaden your awareness. An act of love opens the possibility to see all people as one. The challenge is to recognize which operating system has been activated and take steps to understand why. It is a deliberate practice to become aware of what you're thinking about. Our habitual thinking happens at a subconscious level. The subconscious brain is the part of the brain that allows you to recite the alphabet or drive your car without thinking about all the steps involved. You have performed these tasks so many times that they have become a conditioned routine. The same is true for the never-ending barrage of thoughts that invade our mind, all day every day. We have not been conditioned to pay attention to them.

For most of my life, I mimicked bad behavior. I put others down in order to build myself up. I struggled and faced challenges that seemed unfair. When my spirit was broken, my ego was the first to come riding up to defend me. My ego donned medieval armor and wielded swords ready to knock out anyone who disagreed with me or challenged me.

Instead of blaming someone or something outside of me, I needed to go within and identify my role in my behavior. I was able to identify my familiar pain like I did in the garden, speaking with my mom. I started to ask myself some important questions. What if I could develop a friendship with my fear? What if I could look fear right in the eye and jump off a cliff with it? What if I could embrace my fear and conquer it?

Taking ownership shifted the emotion for me. Understanding where the emotional pain originated allowed me to let go of the victim mentality. With an understanding of the emotional impact of my past pain, I was able to recognize my habitual reactions to it.

MY SOUL CONTRACT

Chapter 17

What If?

Outer chaos sparks reaction. I can see the electrical charge. It is a dull, low frequency. Familiar feelings of fear become activated. I curl up into a protective ball. My arms are wrapped around my head, shielding my ears. My back is curved and turned away in defenseless surrender. Your words travel off your tongue into my heart, and I allow the bitterness to seep into my veins. I recognize your pain in your words.

I begin to unravel. My ears open as I hear you describe your pain within your accusatory words. My back uncurls as I recognize awareness. I turn to you with my heart exposed. I thought your pain belonged to me. My attention is no longer on the bitterness, and I watch as it leaves my veins. My attention is no longer on your sharp tongue, and I watch it retract into your empty mouth. I send compassion to honor your pain. I send empathy to love yourself. I send love to surrender your fear. I send hope to acknowledge your journey.

You are me. I am you.

What if I experienced less pain emotionally, spiritually, and psychologically? What if every choice I made was from my heart and not my head? What if I stopped considering the judgment of others? What if what happened outside of me was no longer a concern? What if I approached every moment from the inside, listening to my inner voice? What if I allowed guidance from the Universe? What if I followed my path regardless of how apprehensive and anxious the unknown feels? What if I tipped the scales of gratitude, abundance, love, and joy in my direction? What if all of this is possible? What if the best part is that it is inexplicably simple?

An internal hurricane forced upheaval and imbalance. That imbalance created a shift in energy. That energy felt so disconcerting and begged for attention. I knew that if I were to ignore this, it would continue to show up until I healed the wound that was holding the negative energy. When healing occurs, a lesson becomes available, and it is as if a light is shining in a dark place. The lessons are here to teach me and to set me free. There were times when I believed I finished the work and that I identified a particular wound. But it showed up again disguised within a different event, making it unrecognizable. When that happened, I knew I had not identified the originating pain completely. There was more for me to learn from a similar emotion, or perhaps the wound was so big it had to be discovered in smaller doses. When I paid attention and did the work, by exploring where the pain originated, I began the healing process. The work of drilling down was difficult because I had to confront my truth. My truth, my ego, is that scared little fuck that would fight like hell to stay protected.

When my excavation was performed with an open heart, and feelings of love, gratitude, joy, and truth were at the foundation of discovery, the answers were simple. Answers were not so simple when my excavation was performed with a closed heart. When I felt the emotions of fear, hurt, betrayal, pain, separateness, hate, and self-limiting beliefs, I was stuck in a victim mentality with limited access to my truth.

Teaching Moment: There is an old saying, "When you point a finger, there are three pointing back at you." This means that while you blame your pain on outside sources, the real cause of the pain is buried deep inside your habitual thoughts. Negative beliefs swim inside old wounds. The original pain looked very different when it was covered up and buried so many years ago. Quite often, your current pain will not resemble the buried pain, and that is what makes identifying it so difficult. In fact, as soon as you're aware of the finger-pointing, recognize that you're blaming something or someone outside of you. Ask yourself, what, in this situation, feels familiar? When have I felt like this before?

Here starts the journey into understanding the root cause of old, buried wounds. Digging to discover the circumstances that created the wall to shield the wound is a crucial factor in understanding current emotional triggers. By becoming the observer of past experiences and recalling the events, without the emotional attachment to the memory, the path to healing has begun.

Stories can manifest into a life of their own. The story's existence requires constant attention to validate the pain that lives inside it. By releasing the attachment to your stories, you can tap into the deep inner knowing of your being. As humans, we choose familiar because it's easy. It's difficult to step back and become the observer of your thoughts and actions because it requires brutal honesty. As a way to cope, we seldom tell ourselves the truth. Our routine emotional reactions are a trained response of subconscious habitual behaviors.

I am learning to heal as I examine my fears and my pain, and with that comes a rebirth of acceptance and self-love. My determination to change supported my choice to establish less stress and invite inner peace. A heightened awareness to begin the practice of a healthy lifestyle was the perfect next step for me.

Chapter 18

Practice, Practice, Practice

My soul is waiting with anticipation as my spirit acknowledges the true path of fulfillment. My spirit feeds my heart with joy and comfort and satisfies the longing of my knowing.

Change is a mindful practice, and making practice a priority brings forth the best results for change. I began introducing daily self-care practices that felt right for me. I believed that if something felt right, held my interest, and offered a benefit that I could recognize, I would incorporate it into my daily routine.

Yoga, meditation, exercise, and a daily check-in were mindful practices I adopted. All of these practices have proven to benefit my personal health and growth. They've improved my overall well-being and have positively affected my mind, body, and spirit.

Exercise was always important to me. In my youth, I was active along with the other kids in my neighborhood. We always had some sort of game going on outside. We played kickball, basketball, and tennis. I played in a softball league every summer, and I loved it. I rode my bike everywhere until I turned sixteen and got my driver's license. I didn't think of riding my bike as exercise at the time, but it was my primary mode of transportation.

Body image became a concern when I entered high school and most likely before that. I remember in sixth grade I was quite *chunky* (a word a handsome man within earshot used to describe me) and I was quite aware of my *chunkiness*. My mom had always struggled with her weight, and the subject of dieting consistently lived in the background of our home. It seemed like someone was always on a diet, except for my dad. My dad, with his six-foot slim physique, maintained an invariable 170 pounds for as long as I could remember. At-home workout videos became popular in the late '70s and early '80s. I purchased them to stay motivated in an attempt to keep a healthy weight throughout high school and in my early twenties. I did not have a weight problem in my teens, but I believed I did. I didn't have a weight problem until after my first pregnancy. During my pregnancy with Nick, I gained fifty pounds and I felt terrific during the entire nine months. By the time Nick was six months old, I had lost twenty-five of those pounds and found out I was pregnant with my second child. As a busy mother of two small boys, I let my exercise routine slip to the bottom of my priority list. I was too exhausted, too busy, and too full of excuses to keep up an exercise regimen. I did make plenty of time, however, to beat myself up about my overweight body. When the kids started school I had a little extra time on my hands, and I became interested in a new exercise video for kickboxing. I could do it in the emotional comfort of my living room, and I enjoyed it. I felt stronger than I had in a long time, and I saw positive results. Unfortunately, because I had inherited the roller coaster diet mentality, my battle with weight continued. Fast forward several years, the boys were grown and I had experienced the traumatic separation with my parents, and my weight was at an all-time high. We had a home gym, and I decided to start strength training. My husband and sons were very disciplined and knowledgeable about lifting weights, so I asked for their instruction and guidance.

I decided at the age of forty-seven that I was going to get healthy the right way. Derrick was instrumental in teaching me about what foods I should be eating, while using weights for exercise. I welcomed a different approach, adopted a disciplined routine, and set a realistic goal of being the healthiest me I had ever been. I found a new determination and used how I felt physically as a barometer for my success rather than the number on the scale. Within a year, I lost fifty pounds and had more energy than I had had in my twenties. At that time, Derrick worked at a popular gym near where I worked, so after much deliberation, I decided to buy a membership. Truth be told, I couldn't wrap my head around the idea that people could watch me workout. I was not a fan of sporting the cutesy workout attire, and I was self-conscious about people judging me.

My gym offered a variety of instructed workout classes. I was interested in the classes that used free weights, cardio, and kickboxing. The classes were held in a glass enclosure which resembled a fishbowl on display. The first time I attended a class, feeling exposed, the gym employees might as well have shouted over the loudspeaker, (in my best impersonation of a corny announcer voice),

Drum roll please . . .

For your viewing pleasure and for all of you who would like to get a load of the gals pumping iron, please focus your attention to the center of the room!

The feeling of being watched and judged slowly faded, and I realized everyone was there for the same reason. It was an environment that proved to offer the challenge I needed, and the instructed classes improved my fitness level and endurance.

My introduction to yoga was on Friday nights at the gym. I anticipated yoga to be the perfect cherry on top of my weeklong workout sundae. I enjoyed the once-a-week experience, and it made me want to learn more about yoga. The following summer, the company I work for rented space to a hot yoga studio in the building next to where I work. Months prior, I had researched hot yoga and scoured my area for classes but couldn't find anything within a practical distance. The yoga studio had not settled into its intended space but held its first few classes in a dance studio in the same building. I was so excited, the class could have been held in the middle of the street, for all I cared.

My first vinyasa class consisted of the instructor, one other gal, and me. I noticed that gym yoga was not like this yoga at all. There were names for poses, and it was fast-paced. I was fascinated and found this type of yoga to be intense and quite challenging. It was not the relaxing, take-me-into-the-weekend yoga I had been participating in at the gym. During my first class, Amy, the yoga teacher, gave me a lovely shoulder massage. At the end of class we lay flat on our backs, and the teacher placed a cool lemon, lavender cloth across my forehead. I was in heaven. SIGN ME UP! I was hooked and soon learned there were many types of yoga, from relaxing and restorative to challenging and invigorating.

Yoga was my first introduction to a meditative experience. Yoga asked me to embrace stillness. It challenged my mind to accept that which is uncomfortable and learn to breathe through it. Yoga taught me how to sync breath to movement and offered a space for gratitude and growth. My yoga practice taught me how to let go of my external environment and turn inward to invite balance and peace. I've experienced some of my greatest lessons in yoga. I awakened to the delicate realization that my inner balance was directly connected to my ability to create physical balance in my postures, or *asanas*. Finding a perfect balance of the mind, body, and spirit was an experience of inner truth and harmony. My yoga practice taught me to overcome myself through the postures. Inviting stillness allowed me to experience a new spiritual awakening. Accepting stillness and having an open mind presented a portal into mystical wisdom. During my yoga practice, I received answers to some of my biggest life mysteries.

I attempted meditation on and off in the beginning of my health and well-being journey. Most of my attempts resulted in frustration. I was physically uncomfortable, easily distracted, full of self-criticism, and I felt as though I wasn't doing it properly. Meditation became easier for me after I was well into my yoga practice. In yoga, I was taught to focus on my breath and nothing else. One of my most memorable and impactful yoga classes was when my teacher, Amy, informed us that we would practice with no music. We were instructed to close our eyes and listen to our classmates' collective breathing while we flowed through the hour-long practice. That, I thought, was what I needed to do in meditation. For me, yoga is a moving meditation, and the struggle *is* the stillness.

With practice, the difficult became manageable, and the manageable became desirable. The desire grew into a practice of letting go of material objects and the physical attachments to my body. My external world became more manageable as I learned to notice thoughts without judgment.

In a chakra workshop hosted by the yoga studio, I was taught a valuable technique about thoughts and judgment. The instructor explained that during meditation, when a thought wanders in, place the thought in a puffy cloud and watch it drift away, and repeat this as often as needed throughout the meditation. This strategy helped me in my meditations and made me realize I wasn't the only one struggling with distractions.

With persistent practice, I learned to limit distractions and meditate long enough to experience amazing things. My meditation practice progressed into a skill that took me to destinations I didn't know existed. I was able to access portals to other levels of consciousness and travel to the vast open universe. The experiences offered a deeply refined definition for me of love and support. Meditation, (which, when translated, means "to become familiar with" or "to know thyself"), taught me how to loosen the grip of outside influences and to release the attachment to my external environment. My familiar environment was filled to the brim with hereditary, habitual behaviors and societal rules. Rules I grew up believing I needed to live by. With continued practice, I was able to open up to a vast expansion of what I accepted as my truth. I embraced a raw passion for my new life and found a connection to the inner workings of my soul and spirit. Meditation allowed for the introduction to and the exploration of my body's energy centers and has transformed my emotional and physical healing. Meditation continues to impact my perspectives as I navigate my soul's purpose while on this amazing journey.

Yoga offered a particular kind of heart-thumping practice for me, but I wanted something more physical. Cardio in the form of running or jogging was not my favorite, and I don't have a runner's physique. I tried it for a while because I was getting bored with other cardio workouts. I set a goal to run a 5k without stopping. I was not concerned with my time and wanted to prove to myself that I could do it, and I did. I don't miss it, and I really don't get the whole running thing, but there are a lot of folks who do. I admire those people and I say, *If you love it, carry on.*

I enjoy walking fast, and I also love to dance! At least once a week on cleaning day, I dance like no one is watching because, well, no one is watching. One day I hope to take some dance instruction, but for now my freestyle is just fine. I noticed that I can't help but smile when I dance; it offers great cardio and it makes me happy.

I adopted a daily check-in routine several years ago, and it has proved to serve me well. No matter how hectic or busy the day gets, I know I have started by paying attention to how I feel and what I need. The practice gives me clear and sometimes shocking answers, but I love a surprise, so I am continually intrigued. The daily check-in asks, *how are you doing?* We ask friends, coworkers, family, and strangers how they are doing, but seldom ask this of ourselves. And I thought about the self-care attitude that I adopted, and I wanted to include a daily practice of self-awareness and self-attention.

I thought about the quizzes I've taken over the years in magazines in an attempt to discover something about myself and laughed as I remembered rigging my answers for the best possible outcome. By bending the truth, I didn't do myself any favors. After all, who cares, it's just me and a magazine. Then that got me thinking, how many times a day do I tell myself that I am fine when I am not? It had never felt natural to pay attention to my emotional well-being. Whether it's a negative or positive emotion, I shove it away somewhere. The negative is just too icky to deal with, and the joy . . . well, the joy feels a bit too undeserving. I am always aware of the *happy gremlins*. They wait in judgment, holding the happy barometer. I can hear their snarky little voices. *Listen to her, she is way too happy. Well, we can't have that now, can we? We must not let her get too cocky; let's have something bad happen to her. That will keep her in check.*

With all of the practices I've developed and adopted, choosing a time of day that worked best for me proved to influence the best overall outcome.

I practice my daily check-in during my drive to work. It's perfect for me because it's after the get-my-butt-out-the-door morning rush and before I'm inundated with office emails and work responsibilities. My commute offers thirty minutes of quiet, uninterrupted time.

I have eight topics I address during my daily check-in practice. I allow the first word or phrase that pops into my head to be the answer. Sometimes the word or a phrase is strange, and I may not know the definition. I find this very interesting, and I make a mental note to remember the word. I then research the definition to analyze the importance and symbolism it might offer. Foundationally, I feel I have paid attention to all of these very important parts of me while it is a great way to honor myself and pay attention to my needs. It offers a great opportunity to express gratitude and set an intention for the day as well.

Teaching Moment for Daily Check-In:

1) **Mind/Thoughts** – Humans have, on average, 70,000 thoughts per day. Of those 70,000 thoughts, 90 percent are the exact same thoughts we had the day before. We unconsciously, obsessively repeat our old stories, day after day after day. Start to become aware of your head chatter and what you are thinking about. Determine whether the chatter is coming from a place of

fear or a place of love. Be as supportive and loving when you talk to yourself as you would a dear friend. Your mind is one of the most powerful tools you have in your well-being arsenal. Because you are a creative, walking, talking genius you have the power to change your thoughts from fear to love. Develop a practice to become aware of your thoughts. Be honest. Be your truth.

2) **Body** – Take a whole body scan. How is your body feeling? Are you fatigued, rested, or sore? Do you have a specific ailment? What is your body asking for today? I have adopted enormous gratitude for my body, acknowledging that it is a glorious mystery. It is strong, and healthy, and the finest, most advanced engineered machine I will knowingly take care of in this lifetime. I am in awe of all that it does for me every second of every day. My body works hard for me, and I don't even have to think about it. When I have to ask my body for something, my body responds. Each day I thank my body for fighting for me. I am grateful for every inch of it, inside and out—every cell, organ, and system. I promise to the best of my

knowledge and ability to fuel my body with nutritious foods from this abundant earth. I respect, honor, and love the incredible vessel I have been gifted.

3) **Soul** – I believe the soul is a borrowed energy onto which we imprint our human experience. The imprint of each human or nonhuman existence and experience stays within the soul for eternity. The soul can be young or old and brings with it many past experiences. It takes up residence in a chosen body for a predetermined amount of time. Our soul is a gift of many past lives, and I believe it is up to each individual to fulfill their intended experiences before the soul leaves the human form. How does your soul feel today? Use the first word that pops into your head. Go with it. I promise it will be interesting. Tap into your soul; ask and receive messages. Opening a dialogue between your thoughts and your inner knowing invites a realization of self.

4) **Spirit** – I believe our spirit is our inner compass, our guidepost, if you will. It is crucial to pay attention to the direction its wisdom offers. Your spirit is your heart speaking to you, that instinctual feeling you get in your gut. Pay attention

and follow the truth of your spirit. It is the leading force that guides you to fulfill and feed your soul's destiny. Use the first word that pops into your head. Go with it. I promise it will be interesting. Listen and allow the true path of your spirit.

5) **Heart** – How is your heart feeling today? Is it huge, open, and full of love? Is it filled to the brim with joy? Is it coherent? Is your heart heavy or light? Is there a hole in it? Is it broken? Pay attention. Thank your heart for all the hard work it does for you each and every day. Ask your heart to be seen today, and let it pour its love onto and into everything you do. You will experience a phenomenal internal balance when your thoughts and actions are in harmony with your heart.

6) **Inner Child** – I have a picture in my head when I speak to my inner child. It is a picture my aunt took when I was about three or four years old, developed in vintage-looking gold and brown sepia tones. I am seated on the floor in a brown-and-white dress with matching fabric suspenders. Beneath the multi-print dress, I am wearing a perfectly pressed white, Peter Pan-collared shirt. My hair is pulled back in a messy ponytail,

and my gaze is fixated on the stuffed animal I am holding. This is me, the young girl I envision when speaking to my inner child. What I've learned through this process is that she is one of the most resourceful truth seekers on my spiritual team. She holds the key that unlocks many of my buried secrets and offers answers to my foundational mysteries. I am forever grateful to have been introduced to her light. Listen and you will be guided. Your inner child is the smartest, most gifted young person you will have the pleasure of meeting.

7) **Gratitude** – I find something to be grateful for every day. Some days are so positive I could name a hundred things. I encourage you to find something different each day to be grateful for. Some days prove to be very difficult, and we all experience those days. If it is a struggle to come up with something to be grateful for, simply be grateful for your breath.

8) **Intention** – Set an intention for the day ahead. Maybe a self-improvement strategy you've been working on or something you would like to start implementing. Perhaps, see the positive in everything you witness today. Or at the very least, try not to have negative thoughts about it. Remind

yourself at different times during the day of your intention, and remain accountable.

All of these practices take training, dedication, and some skill. Like a spiritual athlete, a consistent and constant practice will strengthen your self-awareness. I have made mindful choices to lead a more spiritual life. I have made healthy choices about the food I put into my body. Exercise, yoga, and meditation have proven to be beneficial practices for me. The key is to keep choosing a forward and upward momentum. Sometimes our choices feel out of balance. I believe if we pay attention to the path that feels right in our heart and honors our true spirit, each decision will teach us and lead us to what we need to learn and where we need to be.

Chapter 19

Eliminate the Negative. Accentuate the Positive

I have made choices to eliminate outside influences that no longer benefit me. I am not trying to bury my head in the sand or come across as complacent. I am, however, honoring the fact that I am a highly sensitive person. I am extremely aware of people and my surroundings, and I am easily overwhelmed.

I am much happier if I eliminate the barrage of daily news stories, so I opt out of watching or listening to the news on TV or the radio. I also do not follow, nor am I interested in, politics. Over the last several years, I've made changes by eradicating practices that I can no longer support because they feel negative or leave me feeling drained or empty. I've replaced them by adding new practices that fill me up and bring me joy. I aspire to be aware of what my inner voice is guiding me to do. Because of my new choices, I was already feeling stronger and healthier, and I was beginning to learn what my body liked. But I was aware that there was something more, so I kept following my inner compass.

Ever since I was a young girl, I inherently knew that all we needed to survive and thrive was supplied by this beautiful and abundant sweet Mother Earth. I have long admired cultures with great knowledge of the healing and medicinal powers that plants provide. My focus had been on the food I was eating, and in a natural progression I set about examining other things I was putting into my body.

I opened my medicine cabinet and looked at the shelves lined with white, green, and amber bottles. The prescribed medications I took daily were birth control pills, a drug for my hypertension, and a pill for acid reflux. I ate ibuprofen like it was candy. The rest of the medicine cabinet contained anything I could pop into my mouth to provide quick relief for a plethora of mild ailments. I felt a need to eliminate these medicines. I wanted to follow a more natural, holistic approach for healing, and with some research, I started replacing my prescriptions and over-the-counter regimens with supplements and essential oils.

Some bizarre events led me to go off of my prescribed birth control. My doctor could no longer prescribe birth control to simply prevent pregnancy. He would only prescribe if I had other medical conditions to support taking it. Feeling apprehensive, and remembering news headlines of a fifty something-year-old woman giving birth was enough for me to seek out another health care provider. When I shared my concerns with my new gynecologist, he laughed at me, stating that I was entering the typical age of menopause. I was still having periods, and from my memory of fifth-grade health class, if I was menstruating, I could become pregnant. After two appointments and a thorough examination, my new doctor declined prescribing birth control because I was taking a prescription for hypertension. I decided at that point, that Russ and I would have to seek other options.

At age fifty-one I had my last period, and my gynecologist suggested hormone replacement to help me through the symptoms of menopause. I had no intention of taking any more hormones— after all, I had done that for thirty-plus years!

I then decided to take myself off of my blood pressure medication. I could not understand why my blood pressure had never changed over the course of improving my health. My weight was under control, I was eating right, and yet every checkup was the same. I decided I was going to see if my body would respond on its own to all the good stuff I was putting into it. I purchased a home blood pressure monitor, and I did some research on a supplement that would be helpful during the transition. I informed my husband, friends, and coworkers of my decision to stop my medication just in case it went sideways on me. When I stopped taking my blood pressure prescription, I experienced some weird feelings during the transition. I brought my home blood pressure monitor with me to work, and when I felt strange I would test my blood pressure. I used the monitor to test every morning, afternoon, and evening. I logged all of my numbers and tracked the foods I ate and the types and amounts of supplements I took. I didn't experience any readings from the blood pressure monitor that caused concern. Within three weeks, I was monitoring normal blood pressure ranges on a consistent basis. I am not advocating stopping maintenance drugs, as this can be very dangerous and should be monitored by a physician. My transition was without any concerns, and I felt it would be that way from the start. I somehow knew I no longer needed the medications. Within a couple of months, I took myself off of the supplements as well, and I am still experiencing normal blood pressure.

I chose to cure ailments with natural options from this point on. I learned all I could about essential oils, and I began to use them in place of over-the-counter or prescription drugs. Since I stopped taking my blood pressure medication, and since changing my diet, I rarely get headaches, and my acid reflux and heartburn is nonexistent. Research later revealed that my blood pressure medication was the culprit for my frequent heartburn, after all.

Although I was eating healthy, I wanted more than just healthy, I wanted a preventive alternative. I watched every documentary about food choices and found one that resonated with me. I adopted a whole food plant based lifestyle in March 2015 and have never felt better in my life.

Teaching Moment: I always say, do your own research, try different approaches, and choose what works and promotes a healthy outcome for you. I communicated with my physicians about my holistic choices, and each one understood and was supportive. The best response after an exam for me was, "Everything looks great. Keep doing what you're doing."

A healthy diet is one that fits into your lifestyle, one that makes you feel good and offers the best results for you. The best exercise is the one that you can get excited about and will do consistently. The best meditation is when you offer yourself stillness. The best yoga practice is when you focus on your breath. The best daily check-in practice is when you pay attention to your needs. The best medicine is whatever you believe will cure you. The best food is abundant and is provided by sweet Mother Earth.

Chapter 20

Forgiveness Is Good Medicine

I am a five-year-old sponge, an innocent child, a blank slate.

I sit quietly, absorbing my environment as it caresses my skin and

seeps into my pores. Your words are all I know. Your beliefs are all

I know. Your behaviors are all I know. I idolize you. I worship you.

I want to be just like you. I allow your words to be my words. I allow

your actions to be my actions. I allow your beliefs to be my beliefs.

You would never intentionally hurt me.

I am a potpourri of everything I see and feel. I watch. I pretend. I

mimic. I make excuses. I avoid.

Melting into conformity. I am a perfect mold.

Where did I go?

I have had the honor and privilege to be introduced to many

yoga teachers. My personal favorites are the teachers who are

authentic to their message and, at their essence, are nurturing human

beings. One of my nurturing yoga teachers is Ashley.

It was the end of a Tuesday evening yoga class. All of the participants were in the final resting pose—corpse pose, or as it is often referred to in Sanskrit, final *savasana*. A song played that I had heard once before in Ashley's class. I love Ashley's playlists. Sometimes they are fun and upbeat, and other times they are more serene and soulful. The song that was playing was serene, or maybe I was just that relaxed. Unlike the first time I had heard it, I listened to the lyrics, and by the second verse I was crying. The melody was so moving, and the voice was angelic. I was convinced this was an updated version of a song one would hear in church. As I let the song wrap around me and hold me, my tears released the thoughts of my old self while embracing the new me. Music feels sacred to me. Songs evoke strong emotions and have aided in my healing. Songs transport me back to a special time and place. The melodies and lyrics lift my spirit, make me dance, and console my heart. As I listened, an awareness of my journey became so clear. The path of my journey was paved in forgiveness. I thought about all the teachers in my life and their impactful lessons and how some of my most challenging relationships have offered the most significant lessons for me.

By acknowledging blame as an expression of ego, I've been able to open the corridor to my heart. Once open, I was able to dive inside, feel my way through it, and discover the origin of what or who I needed to forgive. My journey began by forgiving individuals I blamed for my pain and recognizing that they themselves are in pain. Once I honored their pain, it allowed me to embrace empathy for their struggle. I released the toxic relationships in my life and examined the relationships that were no longer vibrating to honor my new energy. Finally, and this was the most difficult, I realized I had to learn to forgive myself.

Forgiveness is true freedom.

As the song came to an end, I made it a point to ask Ashley who the artist was. I wanted to have this song on my playlist so I could listen to the impactful lyrics that were so moving and resonated so deeply. I was surprised to learn that this powerful song "Once Upon Another Time." was from one of my favorite singer/songwriters, Sara Bareilles and was released in 2012. I had never heard of it before. Or perhaps I had never truly listened before.

I've been thinking about certain people and wondering why they are randomly popping into my thoughts. This particular event was difficult to share because it involved so much shame.

The setting is my grade school playground. I estimate that I am about eight years old and in second grade. I don't recall what led up to the incident; all I remember was the name I called a fellow classmate. It is a horrible word. One I learned in my childhood home. A word that I heard from my dad and my grandpa, and it was used in their everyday, normal conversation. It is a negative connotation that was used to describe a certain race. I cannot and will not say it because it turns my stomach to hear the word.

When I was eight, I called one of my classmates this word. I liked Kelvin, so I am not sure why or how this came about. Not that liking him or not liking him gave me any right to say it at all. To say that recalling it made me feel like crap is a huge understatement. *Who the hell am I? Some little white-skinned, blonde-haired, self-righteous, loud-mouthed entitled little shit?* The more I thought about it the more consuming it became. I not only thought about what my act could have meant to this young boy, but I also thought about what happened when he went home and told his mom. *Did he tell his mom? His dad? His brother? How did my act of hatred affect him?* In every aspect of this event, I was a racist and a bully. I thought about Kelvin's mom and dad and what made them decide to put their kids in an all-white school. *What were their circumstances?* Kelvin and his brother were the only two black kids in my grade school. I decided that I needed to apologize for my behavior from so long ago.

I was not on social media at the time, so the avenues for trying to find Kelvin would prove to be difficult, but I wanted to try. I looked online and found that there was a person listed in a town about eight miles from where our grade school was located. I thought it was quite possible this could be the same person. I jotted down the phone number and decided to call Kelvin.

I sat in my car during my lunch break, and I rehearsed a bit of what I would say. I proceeded to dial the number. The phone rang, and my nerves got the better of me and I wanted to hang up. I knew I had to do it right then or I would take the easy way out and not go through with it at all. My stomach was in knots. My call went to voicemail. *Hang up. Hang up. No one will know, he won't recognize my number. Stop. Don't. Don't be a chicken shit.*

The beep . . . "Hi, my name is Micki, (I gave my maiden name). I am not sure if you are the Kelvin I am looking for, but if you attended Central School, I think you are the Kelvin I would like to speak to. I owe you an apology, and if you could call me back, I would appreciate it."

I hung up. My hands were shaking and my heart was pounding.

Later that day, I received a voicemail message from Kelvin. He confirmed that he did, in fact, go to Central School. He offered his cell phone number in case I would like to call him back. I decided to wait until the weekend to call him back.

It was Sunday and Russ was taking a shower. We had planned a day of answering newspaper ads for antique furniture. I found a good seat in the backyard and called the number Kelvin provided. I was even more nervous than the first time I had called. He answered and I introduced myself and thanked him for taking my call. I asked if he could talk for a minute, and he explained that he was at church but he was on his way out the door. I could hear the congregation in the background, and then it got quiet. I told him that I owed him an apology and recounted the events that happened years earlier. He said that he didn't remember the event at all. I told him I was relieved to hear that. Kelvin asked if the purpose for my call was part of a 12-step program. I laughed a little and explained that it was not part of a 12-step program, but it was part of my new personal program. I explained that the event had been on my mind, and I couldn't stop thinking about it. I told Kelvin that I've changed over the last several years, and I needed to apologize. He said, "Well, bless you and thank you."

I thanked him again and told him it was nice to get the opportunity to talk to him after all these years. I wished him well, and we said goodbye. As I hung up the phone, I felt a release. I felt that I had righted a wrong. *Thank God he didn't remember! His folks must have raised a very confident individual.* Now when I think of Kelvin, it is with a memory of doing the right thing. Kelvin honored me with his forgiveness, and in turn I was able to forgive the actions of my eight-year-old self. I went on with my day but couldn't help but wonder how many other behaviors and opinions I inherited from my family and my environment. I had to wonder what else would show up for me on my journey.

Teaching Moment: By following my heart and exposing my shame, I was able to offer an apology for my actions. Forgiveness offered an energetic release. I experienced a release of tension followed by an unexpected inner peace. By paying attention to how I felt in my mind and body, I was able to follow my heart. By acting on what felt right in my heart, I was able to release the stress that was associated with the shame. I have experienced balance in other practices I've adopted, but this was the first time that I felt the balance take place physically. I felt the weight of the actual burden leave my body.

Chapter 21

I Am Sky

Heat punctures my throat while clouds create a fog in my head. Thoughts congest the passageways, narrowing their escape. My teeth ache: filled with words not yet spoken. It is difficult to swallow. Why must I take in what I already know? Instead, it must be shared. Freedom lives in the sharing. Every day feels esoteric, numb and ritualistic, robotic and hollow. My heart is whispering to me, but I cannot hear its prudence. Sending distress for me to consider its motives. Dear Heart, you have my attention. The relief is measured in my body's recovery.

Each step is growth.

This is my therapy. This is my passion. This is my gift.

I am vast, I am clear, I am sky.

With clarity, I sit inside a brand-new day, looking out at the emerald landscape saturated in the predawn rain. I question my disease. I continue to use holistic approaches, including essential oils, teas, and meditation, to soothe my ailments. This morning, my fifth energy center, my throat chakra, is out of balance. The throat chakra is the voice of the body—a pressure valve, if you will—that allows the other energies of the body to be expressed. My symptoms include a scratchy, burning throat, sinus pressure, and tooth pain. My head feels as if it's in a vice, and my ears feel full. I believe, as in so many areas of my life when I listen to how I describe my symptoms, the answers for healing will soon follow.

My ears are full. For me, this means that I have heard enough. It is time to act, and I must speak my mind. Sometimes the fullness occurs because I cannot hear anymore fake bullshit. Oftentimes, when I feel a great amount of pressure in my head, it is a sign that I have to let some thoughts pour out onto a page. It is essential for me to speak through my writing. I've noticed how much more comfortable I am expressing my feelings on the pages of my journals than sharing them out loud. I get strange looks when I share my ideas with people. My journals are safe. People are not. I think back to when my symptoms began. It was after discussing my husband's health issues with him and trying to persuade him to adopt some of my practices. My words are whispers to him, and they created some frustration for me. *Perhaps this is the stress I am feeling, which led me to the symptoms I am having?* I found a guided meditation for the throat chakra, diffused some eucalyptus oil, and wrote in my journal. Within two hours my symptoms disappeared, and I returned to feeling 100 percent.

The following morning, on my way to work, I saw in front and above me a peculiar formation. It resembled the cloud-like exhaust produced by planes in aerial shows. The shape was like an animated, cartoon-like tornado, wide at the top and spiraled down to a point at the bottom. As soon as I saw it, I heard *drill down to ascend up.* The message spoke to me as I was at the heart portion of my daily check-in practice. I had drifted off in my thoughts about feeling an abundance of balanced energy. I had just acknowledged that I felt optimal health physically, creatively, and emotionally.

I felt connected and that connection offered balance during my meditations, my yoga practice, and when I was writing. All of these practices allowed a release of negative energy. For me, the way to release the uncomfortable fullness of the negative energy was to express it through these mindful practices.

There are several poses in yoga referred to as heart openers. While in a pose during Monday night's yoga class, an image came to me. I was in crescent pose, a lunge-type balancing posture. With my back heel lifted, I balanced on my toes, and my hands were together in prayer above my head. With my eyes closed, I bent backward to expose my heart to the Universe. While in the backbend-type pose, the image I saw was a bolt of light that shot out of my chest. The bolt of light created a map inward, inviting my angels and spirit guides to communicate with me. I had never experienced anything so real during my waking hours. The image felt like a mystical download. I was compelled to ask my angels to guide my creativity and bring healing balance. I asked because it felt like I was being presented an opportunity to allow some sort of celestial intervention.

I've experienced fascinating images and curious thoughts during meditation that required interpretation. During those meditations, I've asked higher powers for guidance and help to understand the images, and I've also done my research. From what I've read, some answers come in higher realms of meditation and some from angels and spirit guides. Some of what I've learned I've resisted because fear would not allow me to take ownership of my role. In moments of stillness, I am aware that my spirit is searching to fill my soul's needs, and that offers moments of clarity for me.

Teaching Moment: Learn to become still, and allow your meditations to take you where you need to go. Trust, allow, and surrender to the wisdom, love, and support of the unknown to provide the answers.

We have seven main energy centers in our body. These energy centers can become blocked. These blockages can cause physical symptoms in our body. Meditation is a practice of balancing our body's energy centers to restore a coherent rhythm. Many sufferers can find relief by clearing out stuck energy. Our lower three energy centers are located at the base of our spine, just behind our navel, and at the top of the diaphragm. These lower three energy centers, or chakras, are referred to as your survival centers. They are responsible for holding the emotions related to our family foundation, our connection to others and to ourselves. A healing question to ask while focusing awareness on the lower three energy centers is, "Are my needs being met?" Connection, power, creativity, sexuality, and control reside in these energy centers as well. Guilt, shame, powerlessness, lack, and confinement also live here, just to name a few. The act of balancing these lower three energy centers allows a clear path for energy to move through your body in the lower regions. The upper four energy centers are the heart, the throat, third eye center, and the crown. Once the lower three energy centers are balanced and flowing freely, it is time to bring them up through the heart and dowse them with unconditional love and then to speak your truth using your throat chakra. Next is your third eye center, which is located in between your eyes at the bridge of your nose. It is the invisible eye into spiritual dimensions and represents your intuition or inner knowing. The next energy center is the crown. The crown represents universal consciousness, spiritual enlightenment, and a higher wisdom.

Chapter 22

Dreams

My body is resting. My mind is wide awake.

Splendid communication between the conscious and the subconscious

Epiphenomenon and healing.

Dreams offer answers to the questions in my wide-awake world. Bizarre images beg for attention. Thoughts are energy. Ignored resolution are the dream's energy. I am unable to escape the meaningful mysteries and symbolism.

Curious, animated representation craves my contemplation.

I developed an interest in dream analysis. It seemed a natural progression to adopt a practice to understand the significance of the messages that were brought to me in my sleep. I began to set an intention to remember the details of my dreams before I fell asleep. With a notepad at my nightstand, I was able to record the details when I first woke up while everything was fresh in my mind. Using this process ensured that I could research my dreams' meanings at my convenience. From a literal standpoint, most dreams are quite bizarre. Dreams are the work of our subconscious mind sending messages about our waking life. I was intrigued to discover and understand the hidden meanings within my dreams.

I have a friend, Sarah, I met at work years ago. She is petite, smart, and sassy. I like to describe her as the girl version of my youngest son, Derrick. Perhaps that's why I liked her right away. On one hand she is shockingly raw and hilarious, and on the other hand she is as homegrown and down-to-earth as they come. She is kind and sweet with a strong family foundation, and over the years I have had the good fortune of meeting her parents and siblings.

My dream starred Sarah and her mom.

In the dream, Sarah purchased my sister's house. Sarah was so excited to show it to me, and I was shocked when we entered. She and her husband had restored the home to its authentic 1800s Victorian look. I was impressed with the renovation and how polished and pristine it appeared. As I walked into their main living area, Sarah flipped on the light switch. As soon as the lights were on, all the illusions of my impressions fell away. Everything was as

I remembered it when my sister owned the house but, my demeanor changed as I realized the renovations were a façade. My enthusiasm was crushed and I realized that the new paint was an attempt to hide the cracked and buckled plaster. The wall sconces that appeared to be updated and fastened tightly, became loose and fell to the side as I walked by. Curtains throughout the home were a quick fix to hide a multitude of ill-maintained elements of the house. I couldn't quite understand why Sarah was still excited to show me around. I followed her upstairs and as we entered the hallway, I saw Sarah's mom. We exchanged smiles and Sarah pointed toward the bathroom. I entered the bathroom and saw the bathtub was being used as a litter box. Sarah still had a big smile on her face, so proud to be showing me her new home. I heard Sarah's mom voicing her disapproval of Sarah using the bathtub as a litter box. Upon her mother's disapproval and in a quick attempt to hide it, I picked up a piece of cat feces and put it in my mouth. I spit it out when I realized how distasteful it was.

That was the end of my dream, and of course the most disgusting part for me was eating the proverbial shit. *Quite literally, could it mean that, eating shit?* I came to find out feces has a different meaning in the dream world. Symbolically, dreams about feces may indicate the elimination of the unnecessary and toxic feelings and emotions of shame. The similarities in our families was very telling for me. Sarah's family resembles my own, a family of five with two sisters. Sarah is the youngest of her siblings. The house she bought belonged to my youngest sibling. Sarah represented my sister in this dream, smiling throughout the entire showing of the house, oblivious to her environment. It represented what I wanted to believe about my sister—that she was oblivious to what was going on while we operated the store. When Sarah turned the light on and everything returned to how the house looked when my sister owned it, that image represented my family's behavior regarding facades. *You can hide a lot in the darkness, but turning on the light to recognize the truth, (in this case the truth was the walls, the foundation of our relationship), helped shine a light to see the cracks beneath them.* Sarah's mom represented my mom. Her disapproval of the bathtub being used as a litter box got my attention. As soon as my mom/Sarah's mom voiced her disapproval, it was up to me to fix it. My reaction was to get rid of the thing nobody wanted to see.

Feces represented shame in my dream. I had to hide the shame by getting rid of it. I put the shame in my mouth but spit it out because it was so distasteful.

While deciphering this dream, I realized just how much shame I had swallowed over the years. I shoveled it in and stored it deep inside. I had to make sure nobody could see our shame—after all, if nobody could see it, it didn't exist. It reminded me that growing up was about keeping the veneer sparkly and shiny and making sure everything on the outside looked good. My dream also confirmed the changes I'd made while addressing my shame, acknowledging that I could no longer swallow it in an attempt to hide it.

On a separate night in another dream, I was in a hospital operating room. Toads were jumping all around on the floor. I was concerned for their well-being and shouted, "Don't step on the toads!"

Because of an illness that I was aware of in my dream, my fingers and legs were being amputated. I didn't feel anything as a result of the amputation; I merely witnessed and understood that it was taking place.

After researching the symbolism of my toad dream, I concluded that I was worried about embracing my true self, and worried about squashing my identity. The amputations suggested that I felt limited and questioned my ability to accomplish a demanding task in my waking life.

The messages were clear. I had been struggling with my fear of judgment and my unrelenting relationship with self-doubt. I realized that the only person standing in the way of expressing my true self was me.

The next dream I had during this time was extraordinary. It was, by far, the most vivid and the most palpable. I was standing in what felt like an opening to a cave. The atmosphere was as colorless as the unknown. Heavy, expertly spun webs created a ceiling above me and blocked the path ahead of me. The inhabitants slowly crept into view. At the exact moment I acknowledged their presence, my dream changed from a dull, one-dimensional 1950s black-and-white image to a vivid, three-dimensional, twenty-first-century Technicolor vibrancy. I was in awe as I allowed the animated hues of dynamic colors to surround me. Although the colors beckoned my attention, I had to watch the eight-legged creatures, fearing they would crawl on me or their webs would touch me. In silence, I kept an eye on them, and they kept an eye on me. I wanted to scream and run, but I was patient and still, acting as though I were brave. I watched until the glowing neon yellow and black pair of enormous tarantulas crawled away from me. When they were a safe distance away, I managed to maneuver through the last of the thick, sticky, curtain-like webs. Upon exiting, I found a mirror and stood in front of it, turning and twisting, feeling as though tiny spiders were crawling all over me. I checked my arms, back, and hair for spiders and spider webs. As I turned to face the mirror, the image reflecting back showed my long, dark, wavy hair free of spiders and strands of silk webs, but I had no face.

My findings indicated that to start a dream in black and white and change to color meant that I was looking at a situation from an objective standpoint. The tarantulas symbolized manipulative women in my life. The bright yellow color represented awareness, while black represented passion and intensity. The web symbolized the social network of acquaintances and a desire to control or hold back from expressing myself. The heaviness of the web symbolized my burdens and a need to prioritize responsibilities. The distance I had to travel to get out of the space I was in represented being the odd person out. The mirror symbolized my truth and because I didn't see my face in the dream, that signified the search for my own identity. My dark, long, wavy hair indicated that I was carefully weighing a decision and concentrating on a plan or a situation.

All of the detail and symbolism in the spider dream made perfect sense to me. A week before the dream, I had been struggling with my reaction to an event at work.

At times throughout the years, my work environment often felt more like a drama-induced high school classroom than a professional office. My relationship with two coworkers ran hot and cold. There were times when we all got along and other times when we did not.

My struggle began one February evening. I stayed fifteen minutes late to tie up some loose ends on a project I had been working on. Just as I was about to close out of my email, I noticed a new message had arrived from a female coworker in my department. As I read the details, it became clear that I had been left out of the birthday plans for our boss, the CFO of the company. The email stated that our department would celebrate his birthday the following day. *Why am I just hearing about this now?*

It was common practice for our department to celebrate a birthday by bringing in home-baked goodies and birthday cards. Typically emails were sent out and a date was chosen based on a mutual decision among all department personnel. Confused, I texted my other female coworker (who had already left for the day) to ask if she was aware of the birthday plans. Hoping it was a simple oversight, I explained that the last-minute email from our coworker had not only upset me, but left very little time to bake anything, let alone buy a card. I remember thinking, *I hope I have an appropriate birthday card and a box of brownie mix at home.* Her response was a frigid, "I'm sorry you feel that way."

Her response made me feel like we were back to the cold atmosphere I had experienced from her in the past, although I couldn't think of anything specific that had happened to change what felt like a good working relationship lately.

Birthday celebrations in my department were strange. When I began working for the company, I noticed bizarre behavior around the subject of food and birthdays. The manager who hired me was very particular about who she shared food with and who she would not. One year, while celebrating my birthday, I made a naïve attempt to move the food to the front office area to share with the rest of my office coworkers, but my manager reminded me, "We keep our food back here."

I watched in shock as she marched all of it back to the accounting department.

I found a decent birthday card for the CFO, in my stash of greeting cards, and I left the house early the following morning to stop at the bakery and buy a cake. When I arrived at work, I set the cake down on top of the centrally located bank of filing cabinets in the accounting office.

The coworker I had called the night before (who gave me the cold shoulder) and I were the only two in our department. I sat down to log into my computer and sang a cheery, "Good morning."

There was awkward silence. No response at all.

I opened my email and printed off some invoices that had been sent overnight. A few of them belonged to my coworker, so I attempted to engage in conversation once again. *Perhaps she was busy and didn't hear me earlier*, I thought. I set the invoices in her in-box and said, "Here you go."

Once again, she acted as if I weren't there. *What the heck is going on?* I wondered. I grabbed the birthday card and hurried to put it on the CFO's desk before he arrived. I returned to my desk and opened the birthday email from the night before. I fired off a response and stated that I felt the timing of the email was inconsiderate and left me feeling ill-prepared, and I hoped it would be handled better in the future. Later that day, the men in my department commented on my email, and judging by their responses, they seemed privy to the celebratory details and were not caught off guard as I had been. The female coworker who had sent the email offered excuses and apologies while my other female coworker remained silent. In fact, she had nothing to say to me all day. Each time I joined in a department conversation, she withdrew and became silent.

A week passed and nothing changed at work. An old familiar pattern of mine emerged. I allowed my coworker's silent treatment to affect me in a negative way, and my emotional reaction was an intense feeling of exclusion, hurt, and betrayal. This consumed me, and I had to find a way to release my attachment from it. I tried not to think about it. I wanted to act as if her behavior didn't bother me, but it did. I chose not to ask if something was wrong because in the past, when I asked, she would tell me no and offered no other explanation for her behavior. Asking her opened a door to resolve a situation but asking never changed her overall demeanor. Shoving my reaction down somewhere and ignoring it was not the answer I needed. I had to do the work to understand the pain that had been triggered by her actions and words, or lack of words. In order to let it go, I had to understand the originating emotion that had been triggered. I began the work to drill down and uncover the foundational wound to reveal my truth.

On the surface, the wound felt like betrayal, an emotion that was familiar to me. Using my toolbox, I started to dig for answers and do the work during my quiet commute home each evening. For me the work is the emotional digging and drilling down. It was the same methodical practice I had used on that intense Saturday afternoon when I had the eye-opening talk with my mother.

Each evening as I drove home, I tapped into my memories in an attempt to recall a similar emotional event, a time when I felt ignored and betrayed. I allowed the memories of the separation from my parents to roll through my thoughts. I spoke aloud, which proved to be helpful for me to stay on task, and it kept my thoughts from drifting to the laundry list of things I had to do once I got home. Talking aloud felt like a conversation, and it allowed me to process the emotions associated with the experiences.

I thought about my coworker's reaction the night I texted her about the last-minute birthday email and the following day's events. *Why did I allow her reaction to bother me so much? Why did she shut me out?*

As I pulled into my driveway I said, "She just quit talking to me."

In that moment, the wound, the exposed pain I had been feeling so powerfully during the past week, came to life. I had not made the connection until I said the words out loud. My coworker's reaction was identical to the reaction I had experienced years earlier from my mom and dad.

They just quit talking to me.

After that realization, the next one hit. I was just as much to blame for the outcome by choosing to remain silent. I had gotten the last word by firing off an emotional email. *I yelled and stomped my feet as I ran to my virtual teenage bedroom to sulk and slam the door.*

As I sat in my car, a physical softening occurred. My shoulders relaxed and I felt my forehead unravel and soften.

I was honest with myself and acknowledged my role. My behavior was a replica of what I had observed from my parents. The people who loved me so much had demonstrated the same behavior. I inherited the behavior as if it were my own, with no questions asked. We had become skilled masters. Mom and Dad used it against me, and I used it against them. We fought the same war using the same ill-equipped tools. My parents' reaction, my reaction, and my coworker's reaction were identical.

I got exactly what I needed. I figured out why the silent treatment bothered me so much. I needed the emotional jolt to realize that my coworker was a messenger who held the mirror for me to see my deeper truth.

Teaching Moment: Silence, when used as a weapon, is uncomfortable for me. Being ignored is uncomfortable for me. Paying attention to my discomfort was key in this situation. Although I felt I had done the work concerning the fallout with my parents, my reaction to my coworker proved that the wound had not been fully healed. Part of the wound had been identified and healed, but there was more to learn. The initial lesson learned from my coworker's reaction was that I had not taken responsibility for my actions. Her silence was the mirror I needed to look at myself. I had to understand that these circumstances were simple reminders. Reminders to realize that life will continue to happen, and these glimpses, these events, and these experiences will continually present themselves to me. They will continue regardless of my reaction to them. It is up to me to understand my emotional wounds and pay attention to my reactions. Recognizing my reactions will reduce the amount of time I spend in a reactive period. Remaining in a reactive period for long periods of time causes stress. I am working toward reducing the amount of stress in my life.

Forgiveness was the ultimate gift from this experience. Although I had forgiven my parents, I needed to forgive myself for behaving as if silence were an answer. I was able to acknowledge that I punished the people I care about with silence. That acknowledgment was the lightbulb moment I needed to understand that I could no longer react in this manner. It was a gentle reminder to be mindful of my actions. It will always be easy to choose an old, familiar reaction. It takes practice and self-love to choose a new behavior with a minimal reactive period to ensure a healthy outcome. I will continue to do the work until my easy, familiar reaction is based on my new, familiar, healthy and healed behaviors.

I went to work the following day understanding that my coworker's issues were hers to deal with. I returned with a renewed perspective, forgiving her behavior and honoring a new door of interaction between us. I privately thanked her for the lesson she provided that helped me heal a pain I was holding on to. I granted my coworker and I a clean slate while recognizing a promise to myself. I had a new set of healthy boundaries and an awareness of my emotional triggers that could pull me back to unhealthy behaviors. It became necessary to be conscious of these always.

Chapter 23

Patience and Answers

Elegant and bold, the ebony letters moved harmoniously in front of me. Their orchestrated evolution created powerful words. An orange-feathered quill pen lightly caressed the parchment. The flowing scroll invited a choreographed dance that created magic in my mind.

Ink. Words. Magic. Bliss.

In the spring of 2014, I joined a group meditation class. My experiences in a group setting were very different from what I had experienced meditating privately. In a class setting, the energy was multiplied, making my experiences more intense. This particular class, which consisted of approximately twelve participants— mostly women and a couple of gentlemen—gathered every Saturday morning. Our meditation space was held in a rectangular room in a large office. Each Saturday I was greeted by two women who were licensed social workers. Both women, Lynn and Cheryl, had a welcoming, calm energy about them, and they took turns guiding the meditations. The room had chairs and couches that were arranged in a circle. There were pillows and blankets and tissue boxes dispersed evenly to comfortably accommodate all of us. As I scanned the room and saw the boxes of tissue, I thought, *Do people cry in here? I've never cried after a meditation. Strange.*

The class began with a thirty-minute silent meditation and was followed by a sixty-minute guided meditation. In the beginning, I thought ninety minutes seemed quite a long time to meditate, but I was always surprised by how quickly time passed. It was in these classes that I learned how to leave my external world behind in order to be introduced to my internal world. With Lynn and Cheryl's guidance, I learned to invite stillness, focus on my breath, and allow a relaxed state of deeper consciousness. I remembered one particular meditation in December, when my meditation proved to be quite profound.

I had entered what felt like a hypnotic state and watched as a scene played in front of me like a movie. The trance-like feeling numbed my entire body. I was unaware of where I was or who I was. I felt comforted as I traveled further and further into the unknown. I was the observer, experiencing awe-inspiring information. I was captivated and knew I was receiving an important message through unspoken words. I understood the importance of the message.

The instructor's voice had left my ears. The scene that played in front of me was a stunningly animated, private viewing. My attention was solely on what was happening in my mind. Floating weightless in total darkness, letters of the alphabet, in the fanciest handwriting I had ever seen, began to float by in front of me. As I watched the synchronized movement, the letters began to form words beneath an orange-feathered quill pen. The end of the feather was dipped in black ink, and it made an audible scratch as it danced along the parchment. In full view now, I watched as it moved methodically over an elongated scroll of paper. A lullaby played softly in the background, and I was in a place of emotional bliss. I was content. Words. Paper. Ink. There were no voices and no audible directions. I experienced a simple knowing. I experienced an understanding that what I was shown would be my sanctuary and my therapy.

A soft voice interrupted. It was our instructor asking us to come back into our breath. With instruction, she led us back to our physical realities and our physical bodies. We opened our eyes, and after a few moments, we were invited to share our experiences. A woman seated across from me was the first to share and, I listened as several more shared their fascinating experiences. I felt vulnerable when I decided to share, but I also felt supported by this group. I focused high on the wall across from me as I described where I went and what I experienced. It wasn't until I stopped talking and lowered my head that I realized I couldn't recall one word I had said. I had experienced such a deep, almost hypnotic state that I think I was still coming out of it while I told my story.

That particular meditation offered an amazing connection to a deeper sense of self. It was a heartfelt glimpse into a higher vibration and to a special place within. This higher consciousness opened a connection to a place where my dreams existed and my creative expression was waiting to be discovered.

Teaching Moment: After experiencing that meditation, the importance of bringing that feeling into my everyday life was paramount. I wanted to experience more of this unknown realm. I wanted to become very familiar with it. After sharing with the group, I learned that I could be vulnerable and still be okay. I was able to speak my truth with confidence. I learned to use my meditation experience to help understand my waking life and my nighttime dreams.

This experience gave me the courage to share my secret passion with my family.

Chapter 24

Secret Revealed

It was Christmas Eve 2014, and we had finished our holiday meal. We cleaned up the kitchen and, as was customary in a long line of Abels tradition, opened all of our gifts. Each of us attempted to organize the unwrapped boxes and oddly shaped objects into uneven towers next to where we sat.

As I looked at my boys on this Christmas Eve, I thought about how alike and how different they are and how proud I am to call them my sons. They both are sweet, sensitive, honest, hard-working, strong and confident. Nick is smart and more serious but has a great sense of humor. He embraces a challenge. He is a good listener and is diplomatic. He is a kind and gentle soul. Derrick is smart and has a quit wit and is genuinely funny, he brings humor into almost everything he says or does. Derrick keeps us laughing and likes to bring some shock value into a conversation. Derrick can navigate a challenge and hold his own in a debate. He is a kind and gentle soul. I am lucky they chose me to be their mom.

Russ and I, Nick, Nick's girlfriend, Christa, and Derrick were feeling relaxed as we stared at the only lights in the room. Hundreds of mini white lights swirled around and illuminated each heirloom ornament on the branches of our well-loved Christmas tree. It was late and the room was sufficiently overflowing with stuffed bellies and full hearts. The warm scent of the balsam candle filled the holiday air. I breathed in the love of my family and our comfortable traditions. I was grateful to share Christmas Eve with my favorite people in the world, and everything felt supremely perfect in that moment. With Russ, Nick, Derrick, and Christa gathered together, it felt like the appropriate time to share my secret. The one I had kept in my heart for so long.

I nervously shared, "As long as you're all here, there is something that I want to share with you. I have been thinking about writing a book."

I paused with the anticipation of confused expressions on my family's faces. I had rehearsed how and what I would say about my secret. In my rehearsal, I had pictured my husband teasing me. In my rehearsal, I thought that once my secret left my lips, the boys might utter some sarcastic comments, but there weren't any. I had their attention, and no one uttered a teasing word or made a face. I was seated across the living room from Nick, Christa, and Derrick, and they looked genuinely interested in what I had to say. I looked at my husband, relaxed in his favorite recliner as he grinned his supportive smile and nodded his head. That was my cue to continue.

I shrugged my shoulders and looked back at the kids, and I heard, "That's cool," "Interesting," "That's neat."

And then Derrick asked, "What is the book going to be about?"

I hadn't anticipated anyone being interested enough to ask me that. I stumbled around for a moment, contemplating how I wanted to answer.

"It is going to be a true story. My story. It will be about my life and what I went through after the separation with my mom and dad and your aunt and cousins. I'll outline my journey and my spiritual transformation. I want my book to help someone who's struggling. My intention is to share what I've learned through my experiences. If I can help someone, I'll feel as though I have fulfilled a purpose."

I felt exposed yet supported. My secret was out, and not one of them was laughing! With all my rehearsing, I had set myself up to believe that if they weren't interested I would be let off the hook. The idea of writing a book, which seemed like a huge undertaking, could be released by their disinterest. But instead, they were intrigued and curious about my idea. Their receptive responses shifted what felt like a desire I could have easily given up on, into the dream I had to pursue.

Their loving response shifted my intention of wanting to write a book to having to write a book. I had to prove to them that my dream would be a reality. I felt like they had just handed me the golden ticket to board the Go-For-It Express. My family had granted me their blessing with no judgment and no expectations. They had an honest curiosity about something that interested me. At that moment, I was grateful as each of them unwrapped their hearts, acknowledging that I would be exposing our shared hurt and pain. For the private family I knew we were, this would prove to be quite a change for us.

As I lay in bed on that Christmas Eve, I thought of the years behind us and the ones in front of us. I thought of all the things my boys had to look forward to in their lives. As their mom, I always thought of their well-being. *Are they happy? Are they following their dreams? Are they healthy? Are they safe?* From the day I met my husband to the day my children were born, my attention has been on the three of them. My heart burst with pride as I thought of the people they had become, and I wondered what secret dreams lived in their hearts.

They have shown me time and time again their strength, their depth, and their honesty. I know they are caring and sweet, funny and serious, and I adore everything about them. I will never stop being their cheerleader. Yet, when I shared my dream, I didn't expect them to be my cheerleaders. I thought about how the tables had turned. All I ever wanted was to be a wife and mother. I will forever be honored to have earned those titles. But there was more for me. The most important people in my life had presented me with the best Christmas gift ever. Their love and support was the shiny red ribbon that tied the gift together. All I had to do was pull the ribbon and open the gift. The gift was the freedom to pursue all that was waiting for me to discover.

It was the morning before New Year's Eve, and I watched my oldest son, Nick, with his girlfriend, Christa, prepare to leave our home after a well-spent holiday visit. They were unaware that I was watching them. The TV monitor acted as a mirror, reflecting their images from the back bedroom down the hall. I was overcome with pride as I watched the man Nick had become. He has a kind and gentle heart. He is confident and brave, sweet and headstrong, just like his dad. I allowed my thoughts to transport me back to when he was a little boy and the day we decided to buy this house for our growing family. I thought about our family of four and how I dreamt of being a family of five. I watched the two of them and thought about the many years my family has spent inside our home. I thought about the four walls of this home that have kept our secrets and have been infused with my family's stories of love and joy, sorrow and pain. I was overcome with emotion as I watched my son with his best girl, secretly knowing she would be the one I would call daughter someday.

I just may have that family of five after all, I thought. *Maybe more. Lucky me.*

With the holidays over, Russ returned to work and the kids returned to their lives. I had one day left of Christmas vacation to enjoy in tranquil solitude before I returned to work. The house was quiet, and I spent the morning in front of the woodburning stove. The warmth of the fire penetrated my bones, and the aroma of fresh-brewed coffee calmed my senses. I wrapped my hands around the oversized mug and pressed it against my chest. I felt warm on the inside as I turned my attention outside. I watched the oversized flakes of snow that started to fall in front of the window. I watched as each one accumulated to create a pure white cold carpet on the ground outside, and I was grateful. Wrapped in a blanket, I sat back on the couch to enjoy my view. The quiet inside combined with the beauty outside provided a perfect combination to turn inward and pay attention to myself. I had gotten out of my usual routines during the holidays, and it dawned on me that I hadn't done a daily check-in for a few days.

I began my morning ritual and put my awareness on my mind and my thoughts. I allowed feelings of enormous gratitude for the time spent with my family to seep in. I allowed my thoughts to float over the past few days, and I smiled as I recalled our time together. I stayed in those thoughts as I took another sip of coffee. Next, I brought awareness to my body. I recited the usual affirmations: *I am grateful for my strong, healthy body. I am grateful for all the organs, tissues, systems and cells of this body. I am grateful for my heart and my lungs, blood and bones. I am grateful for all of the parts that work so hard to maintain a healthy me. I am grateful for the vessel I have been blessed to walk around in.*

I stopped because I was distracted by another thought. A truth that wouldn't allow the last thought to be 100 percent accurate. I began to fixate on the fact that I had gained fifteen pounds over the course of the past year. The thought pulled me out of my meditative state. I thought about how I felt the extra weight. I felt it in my yoga practice, I felt it in my clothes. I felt a lack of control because I knew it was a conscious decision to make healthy choices, just as it was a conscious decision to not make healthy choices. I knew I should step away from the negative chatter, but in my depths I was struggling. *Why? Why am I so hard on myself? I hate this struggle. Damn this behavior.* I asked the questions. I sat and allowed myself to feel the inner turmoil, the letdown, the disappointment in myself. Then I thought about judgment. *Am I struggling with self-judgment or the judgment from others? What am I afraid of? Judgment from other women? Judgment from my husband?*

Russ knows I've struggled with my weight my entire life. There were times that I felt my weight bothered him. So much so that I pulled away physically and emotionally. He noticed things I did to cover up my body in our most intimate moments. He gently nudged me to explain my mannerisms. I seldom experienced moments when I felt safe enough to be vulnerable and share my most self-deprecating thoughts with him. As I allowed a memory to wash over me, I was reminded how lucky I was to have a husband who tells me that I am beautiful every day.

As I sat in front of the warm fire, I recalled a special memory. Russ and I were lying in bed. His hands were gently caressing my body. He was staring at my belly while his hand made a circular motion, allowing his fingertips to brush across my abdomen. It tickled, but all I could think about was that he noticed the weight I had gained, and he was calling attention to it. Because I felt self-conscious and ashamed, I pushed his hand away.

He looked at me confused and asked, "Why did you push my hand away?"

I answered as if he knew what I was thinking. "Because."

He coaxed, "Because why?"

I rolled my eyes as I realized he was going to make me say it. I scanned my body for all of its imperfections. I looked at the stretch marks that appeared during my first pregnancy, faded but still present. A constant reminder that even if I had kept the weight off, I would never wear a bikini again. I looked at my belly button and how the depth of it changed depending on the amount of fat around it. I looked at the flat space between my breasts because gravity had pulled my boobs into my armpits.

As I leaned forward to pull the sheet over my body, I said, "Because it's gross."

Russ looked deep into my eyes and said, "Don't *ever* cover up your body."

He placed his hand on my belly and looked at it and said, "Don't *ever* feel bad about this. This is the place where you carried my babies. This will always be a very special place to me. Please don't *ever* feel bad about that. You are a mom, you are a miracle to me because you were able to do that. So don't ever feel ashamed of this, please."

He gave me the sweetest kiss and hugged me with such tenderness, and I melted into his loving arms. Between his heartfelt words and obvious emotion, I couldn't hold back my tears of gratitude. As I lay with my adoring husband, I realized how my self-sabotaging lack of confidence allowed me to narrowly guess what he was thinking. Because this man could read me so well and begged me to be honest, I received a much-needed reminder of how lucky I was to be in the sweetest place on earth with the sweetest man on earth.

As I continued to stare at the fire burning and the snow falling, I urged myself to dig a little deeper to understand what lay underneath my behaviors of self-sabotage. I vowed to pay more attention to patterns of learned behaviors and understand why it was so easy to fall into those familiar routines. I finished my daily check-in, and it felt good to be back on track. I made myself a promise that morning. I promised to be gentle with myself and to look at my body as the miracle it is.

Teaching Moment: Winter offers more hours of darkness than sunlight, a perfect cocktail for quieting the mind. The brain reacts to darkness by increasing the dose of melatonin. This hormone invites the body and the mind to become quiet and still. When I quiet my mind and my body becomes still, I am able to pay attention to my inner voice and my inner light. I can see everything I am grateful for. I have the love and support of family and friends. I have the ability to see through the veil and expose my truths. Hard lessons have taught me to be inherently keen about who treats me well and who does not. I am grateful to share myself and my dreams and to be vulnerable with family, friends, and loved ones who have earned the right to hear my stories, my dreams, and my desires.

During my morning check-in, I was reminded that honest communication is so important. I was so involved in my own negativity and shame that I couldn't allow the possibility of a different observation. I was reminded how lucky I am to have a partner and friend who loves me and encourages me to acknowledge, honor, and recognize my true feelings. I am blessed to have a person in my life who shows me and tells me that I am valued and lovable. People treat you the way they want to be treated, so this forced me to ask an important question: *Why am I not sharing with him my deepest heartfelt thoughts about him?* He deserves to hear wonderful things about his body and how attracted I am to him. He deserves to hear how much I love being with him, even if we are sitting quietly in the same room. He deserves to hear that I feel safe in his presence. He deserves to hear that I still feel like an infatuated teenager when I crawl into bed with him. He deserves to hear that when he hurts, I hurt; when he is in pain, I am in pain; and when he is happy, I am happy.

I have struggled with this type of honesty. Fifteen years ago, when I spoke my truth to my folks, when I exposed my true feelings and bared my soul, I made my heart vulnerable, and they turned away from me. My honesty was met with betrayal, so I remained guarded for a long time. On that cold January day, I realized I have taken some things for granted. I need to make the effort to share my true feelings with the people who deserve to hear them. I would not want to die tomorrow not having shared my heart with the people I

love and care about.

Chapter 25

Brylcreem, Turpentine, and Old Spice

I sit with my elbows resting on his workspace. My chin rests in my hands, and my feet dangle off the stool. I watch my grandpa work. The blend of pungent aromas remind me that I am in his garage. Turpentine-soaked paint brushes line the edge of the table. Brylcreem held all but one strand of his dark locks in place. The soft scent of Old Spice lingers and sits on top of the smoke-filled air. Giant hands move with meticulous, artistic perfection along the blank canvas.

I am happy. I am safe. I am loved. I am supported.

I called my grandpa Papa, and as I thought about him, I was instantly transported to his garage. A space that was not used as a garage at all but rather an art studio where he worked on his many projects. My mind wanders and I am seated across from him as he works. The melancholy aromas are a heartwarming combination of Old Spice, Brylcreem, turpentine, and tobacco smoke. Papa was a dead ringer, both in looks and charisma, for Clark Gable's character in the movie *Gone with the Wind,* but Papa's build fit a much larger German frame. We are encapsulated among the clutter with just enough room for the table he worked on and a chair on either side. His one car-sized workspace on Marquette Place overflows with paint cans, paintbrushes, new canvases, pieces of wood and turpentine-soaked rags. As I sit and breathe in the bouquet of aromas that are my grandpa, I am happy to be in his presence. Brylcreem holds all but one piece of his dark locks in place. A newly lit cigarette is balanced in the corner of his mouth. His head is tilted to the right as his caring, pale blue eyes squint against the smoke as it swirls and drifts toward the wooden rafters, left to marinate in that garage forever. A 1960s-style radio sits behind him on a shelf; it isn't on, but he sings. His melodic baritone fills the space and makes me feel safe. His giant hands, covered in splashes of color, guide the paint-filled brush in strokes of precise artistry.

My grandpa was patient and kind. He was soft-spoken, and I don't recall ever seeing him upset or angry. I felt as if I spent many summer days with my grandpa, watching him work in that garage. Maybe it was a lot of time, maybe it was not. Regardless of the amount of time I spent with him, he left an impression on me. I am infused with peace and calm as I inhale the magical mixture of fond memories of my grandpa.

These familiar aromas surprised me when they invited themselves to my next yoga practice. As I laid in final savasana, my thoughts drifted towards self-doubt and lack. Although I had received positive reactions about writing a book from my family, I began to doubt my writing skills. I believed what I told myself for years as I compared my lack of artistic talent to that of my mom, sisters, grandma, and grandpa. I recalled acknowledging that I didn't get the artistic gene. In my next breath, my concerns increased as I thought about my grammar, punctuation, prose and content. *I better take an English class or a writing course.*

As I became consumed with thoughts of why I should abandon the idea of writing, I smelled the aromas that reminded me of my grandpa. I was elated as the sweet scents became stronger, making me feel as if I opened my eyes, Papa would have been seated right beside me. Just then I felt his presence, bringing me so much comfort and peace.

Then I heard his deep voice whisper, "Your pen is your paintbrush and paper is your canvas. You sculpt your artistry by molding a healthy mindset. Your passion is your gift. Your words are your heart's expression. Your art looks different than mine, but you, my dear, got the gene."

In final savasana, receiving a message of support from my beloved grandpa felt safe and admittedly, a little weird.

I felt my mother-in-law, Laverne Abels' presence as I drove to work the other morning and spotted yet another brown couch. *Rural Illinois is apparently running rampant with abandoned brown couches*, I thought to myself. A brown couch was the symbol I had asked Mom Abels to show me to confirm that we were in direct communication with one another. When I spotted the brown couch, I thanked her for acknowledging that I had been thinking about her. I allowed my thoughts to drift, and I thought about our many conversations and the many memories I had of her. She had a welcoming presence, and I felt safe and supported when I shared my life with her. I missed our honest conversations, and I missed being in the presence of a sweet, caring, and nurturing woman.

Mom Abels and I shared many heartfelt conversations, and with each one, she offered her love and grace. One of her traits that I found so endearing was that she never judged another person. She was in my life for eight short years, but in that time, she shared her compassion for others while living with her own tragedies. During our conversation, she gave me her full attention, and she listened to me. I wasn't shy around her. I wanted to learn from her and be like her. I didn't realize the gifts she had given me back in the 1980s, but I know now and I thank her often for them. She left the physical world over thirty years ago—much too soon—and only one year into my marriage to her son. My sons never got the privilege of meeting their maternal grandma in the physical world, but I know she held each of my babies before I did. I know she guided their souls to Russ and me, and I know that her spirit continues to watch over all of us. Although she couldn't physically sit at the baseball games or share meals on Sundays or share a toast during the holidays, I know she was always present. She was there to help guide her husband on his journey to join her fifteen years later. Her love always surrounds us. Her comforting ways and warm heart continue to bring us peace in our losses and calm our hearts when we struggle along the way.

Mom Abels has come to me many times with guidance and answers since her passing. One time in particular, Russ and I were pulling away from each other, and our relationship was suffering. I felt I had exhausted all of my avenues. Nothing seemed to be working, and I had run out of answers.

During yoga, I had allowed the troubles Russ and I were experiencing to wash over me. During the final resting pose of the evening's practice, I silently confessed that I didn't know what to do. I asked Mom Abels for her help, guidance, and wisdom. She came to me, and I could not only feel her presence, but I could actually see her. Her face was on the right side of my face, nestled between my shoulder and my chin. Her presence had an immediate effect and calmed my spirit.

She answered by whispering three simple words: "Just love him."

She left as quickly as she appeared. Her physical presence was undeniable. I broke down in tears as I let the realization of her visit surround me. The moment felt so private, and even though I wanted to share my bizarre experience, I knew how crazy it would sound. The reality suited her personality perfectly. My trusted, beloved mother-in-law offered a simple answer in an intimately private setting as she always had. She presented the answer wrapped with her love and truth and hand-delivered it from her heart directly into mine.

Teaching Moment: When the doors to spiritual guidance are open, you will be amazed at how the answers reveal themselves in a blend of real and surreal experiences. I believe, therefore I receive. We are all born with intuitive gifts. We are born with a curious nature. I am amazed by the profound experiences since becoming more and more curious. As children, we are born naturally clairvoyant, which, by definition, literally means "clear vision." As we age, we may not pay attention to or hone in on our own psychic abilities. As our attention and our curiosities fade, our psychic development fades as well. I've discovered that, at any age, if you tune in, you will rediscover your inherited birthright. We all possess intuitive gifts. Personally, it wasn't until I became very still and was able to quiet my mind enough to allow something that had always existed to reenter my life. Like all things, this, too, was a practice. With guidance, I was able to further develop my intuitive skills. Prior to feeling my grandpa's presence and receiving his message of support, my sense of smell was intuitively activated making me feel as if he was physically present. I learned that I possess the gift of clairalience, (the ability to smell odors that don't have any kind of physical source). I'm sure you have had experiences that you cannot explain. Perhaps little happenings that make you think of a loved one who have passed. Maybe the dearly departed randomly pop into your thoughts, or you see an object that reminds you of them, or you experience déjà vu. It's easy and almost automatic to shrug these experiences off as odd. You might continue with your daily routines, never exploring the reasons why this happened. Perhaps someone is trying to get your attention, communicate with you, send a message, or provide guidance. Stay curious and explore. Open your heart to receive spiritual messages. Trust that spirit wants what's best for us. Ask and be open to receive the gifts.

Chapter 26

With Age Comes Doubt, With Wisdom Comes Freedom

I'm struggling. I'm tired. I'm tired of doing the work. The work is never-ending. I need a break. I'm overwhelmed. I'm questioning the payoff and the end result. Is there an end? Why do I put myself through the turmoil and difficulty? It was so much easier when I was oblivious and unaware, when I was clueless about my spiritual path. It's too much sometimes, it's just too big.

I try to go back. Back to where I existed before. Back to my naïve, unevolved self. I tried not to care anymore. I tried. As difficult as the work felt at times, it was better to continue on a forward momentum. Going back felt like a huge disappointment. Going back felt like a dishonor to my soul. Overwhelmed, I remind myself to breathe. I invite myself back. I invite the wisdom I have gained thus far. I invite more lessons.

I need.

I need to be gentle and kind to myself.

Take a break. Take a breath. Take time and return.

It was January 2016, and I was questioning why all of this spiritual work appealed to me at all. I felt as though it was nothing but a gigantic puzzle. I hate puzzles. My work, my journey, involved taking each little piece of my emotional puzzle and figuring out where it fits in to this thing called life.

There was drama in the background at work. *Maybe that's part of it*, I thought. *I'm worried because there are rumblings about layoffs.* I wondered if I would be let go. I started to wonder if my age and my outdated abilities were no longer valuable. I started to wonder if the aggressive, college-educated, go-getters were more desirable than I was. My mind raced: *Why do I allow myself these moments of self-loathing, self-talk? I know better. I am what I am, and just because someone I work with decides to go to school to earn a degree or takes on more responsibility to prove their worth doesn't mean I need to feel less than.*

In reality, I have been in each of those positions before, and it proved, with grim reminders, that neither was a good fit for me. I remembered the days of putting work first and family second. That arrangement never felt good. It never felt right for me or my family.

I had hoped for fulfillment in my career. I was and am not that girl. My fulfillment comes from my connection to people, namely my family.

After honoring my truth, I reminded myself that with age comes wisdom. I had the backbone to admit honestly and with integrity what works for me and what does not. Drama does not work for me. Dog-eat-dog aggressive work attitudes no longer work for me. A certain degree of confidence would serve me well in dealing with some technical issues; however, I am not that interested in advancing my computer skills beyond my everyday use. That being said, I am perfectly adapted to handle my current work situation, and I can quit beating myself up about my lack of having been an aggressive twenty-something. I've decided I will observe from my well-experienced surroundings and embrace my personal contentment.

A few days later, my dear friend Heidi stopped by to give me a birthday gift. I love and admire Heidi. We have been friends for over twenty-five years. She is the family I chose. I love her camaraderie, loyalty, and support. She is bubbly and exuberant and has always made herself available to hold space for me. Her friendship is a gift I will always hold in my heart. I am grateful for her sense of humor and her ability to offer guidance. Heidi has been one of my cheerleaders and has held me accountable to continue pursuing my dreams. I plan on growing old alongside her, knowing that we are going to be cool old ladies together.

Heidi's birthday gift to me was a bright pink purse. Choosing a bright spring color in the middle of January proved just how well my friend knows me. I tend to dress in bright colors on gloomy winter days, and bright pinks and oranges can absolutely squash the winter blues for me. As I accepted her gift, I set the purse on my wood dining room table and heard the little brass feet make contact with the hard surface. As soon as those brass feet hit the table, my head filled with memories. *Oh my God, am I the age that my purse has little feet just like my Great Aunt Ceal's and Great Aunt Mary's?* I giggled silently and shook my head, trying to rinse the images that were igniting my nostalgic thoughts. Trying to control the lengthy explanation of my memories, I focused on opening gifts that filled each of the purse's three divided compartments.

Heidi would have relished in my giggles and understood the impact of my corny memory, but I refrained from sharing because she had a full evening planned. She stopped by with her son and daughter, and they were on their way to meet her third and eldest daughter for dinner. I didn't want to take up her time with my heady nostalgia.

Aunt Ceal and Aunt Mary were sweet women on Dad's mother's side of the family. Ceal and Mary had "hi Jane" arms, sweet personalities, and huge purses that resembled miniature pieces of 1950s luggage. Their purses held plenty of tissues and good intentions. I fondly recall the aunts waving goodbye with their flabby under-arm flaps swaying back and forth.

My new pink purse was just like theirs, and on my fifty-fourth birthday, I sure didn't feel how I remembered my great-aunts looked. Perhaps when my great-aunts were fifty-four, they thought that too. I hope they did!

Teaching Moment: I allowed myself to be concerned with what someone younger than I viewed as an important work advancement. And although I would enjoy making more money, I am not interested in continuing my education in accounting. I fell into this line of work because I am a self-described numbers girl. I am good at math, and my mother taught me bookkeeping years ago, and it has served me well. The difference, I realized, is that although I am not opposed to learning new things, I've decided that the new things have to get me excited. I am constantly and continually learning. The difference is my attitude about learning. If I honor my intuitive curiosity, I will learn about what interests me. I believe if I remain curious and continue learning, it will lend itself as one of the all-time age defiers. My hope is to never lose my can-do assertiveness or the belief in myself that I have wisdom to share through understanding the grace that came out of all my life experiences.

I thought about the knowledge we have available to us at our fingertips concerning our health and well-being. We are so lucky to easily pursue information and adopt an aggressive approach to embrace a well-balanced lifestyle. So many have made their mental and physical health a top priority. I applaud us all.

Chapter 27

Dancing and Celebrating

I sway and allow the music to move me. I invite the melody to seep into my being. The rhythm moves my shoulders and my hips, and I'm gone. As my feet glide across the floor, I close my eyes and I am transported to happiness. The joy lifts the corners of my mouth and fills my heart.

My smile broadens my energy field, and I dance like nobody's watching.

One of my most freeing experiences took place at a holiday party hosted by the company I worked for back in 2010. Although I had no clue it was a spiritual lesson at the time, I am able to recognize that I followed my heart, and created my own joy.

Our company parties never disappointed. The parties always had enjoyable entertainment, top-shelf liquor choices, wonderful food, and great music. Most of our company parties had a theme.

For this particular party, every employee and their guest were invited to dress in their favorite '80s attire.

I have always enjoyed themed parties, and I had fun finding a costume online that was perfect for the evening. I looked like a cross between Madonna and a Valley girl wannabe. My holiday outfit was black and neon green with black lace gloves and a matching headband with a black lace bow. Knee-length black leggings were accented by a black leather bustier that fit over a black opaque top. The waist was cinched with an oversized black belt that separated my leggings from the neon green-and-black tulle skirt. The outfit was complete with a matching pair of neon green-and-black striped leg warmers that sat on top of black boots. The outfit was fun, and I was ready to have fun.

Russ does not share my enthusiasm for parties. Years ago we made an agreement concerning my love for social events and his lack of love for social events. I understood that he didn't enjoy the crowded party atmosphere and I would not nag him about it. He understood that I loved parties and would go, guilt-free, without him.

I love to dance. I get my cardio in and get a great workout both physically and mentally every Saturday while I blare my music and clean the house. I used to dance all night when I was younger and couldn't have cared less about what anybody thought. The older I got, the more self-conscious I became. After each of our company parties, while I drove home, I wondered why I allowed myself to sit in a chair all night while I watched everyone else dance the night away.

It was Saturday and it was holiday party day. I dressed in my '80s outfit and felt great. On my way to the venue I told myself that I was not going to be concerned with others' judgment. *I am going to dance the first dance and not leave the floor*, I decided.

Our dinner was over, and the DJ was all set up and ready to play. The first song of the night was "Hey Mickey." My coworkers at the table next to me were trying to get another coworker onto the dance floor. I was chair dancing at my table while enjoying their antics. *I'll go to the dance floor as soon as someone else goes*, I said to myself. I stood up, and the people at my table started singing and pointing at me.

"Hey, Mickey, you're so fine . . . Come on, Micki, go dance."

As soon as I saw the guy at the table next to me head toward the dance floor, I decided to take the plunge and go to the dance floor too. My boots hit the hardwood, and my skirt flared out as I spun around. I danced with my head down because I knew if I saw anyone watching me I would run back to my safe, boring chair. The room became very loud with whistling and yelling. I wondered what I was missing, so I turned around to see who they were making all the noise about. I saw the guy who was headed up to the dance floor right behind me, standing at his table, clapping along to the song. In my peripheral vision, I was aware that no one was on the dance floor on either side of me. As I spun around another 180 degrees, hoping to see someone else on the floor, it became clear that I was the only one on the dance floor. For a moment, I was embarrassed and my head wanted my legs to run off the floor and into the ladies' bathroom. I am not sure why it worked, but with all the hootin' and hollerin', watching my friends with big smiles on their faces, screaming the lyrics to "Hey Mickey" kept me on the floor. Before the song ended, I had some company on the dance floor, and I followed through with the promise I made myself. I stayed on the dance floor all night (except for the slow songs), and I had a ball.

Teaching Moment: The one thing keeping my butt in a chair all that time was the debilitating fear of judgment. By making a promise to myself and keeping it, I was able to overcome what had become a fear. *Everyone has a camera with them at all times now. What if they take a picture of me and post it on social media and make fun of me?* Thinking like that had allowed my ego to make the decisions. Defensive ego, afraid of getting hurt kept my feelings safe. If I would have stayed in the chair, I would have pleased my ego, but I would have gone home once again, asking myself, *"Why?"* Instead, I looked fear in the face and said, *I don't care. This is me, and I'm okay with that.* It was a newfound confidence. And I hoped perhaps that confidence would help me get my husband on the dance floor at our friend's wedding, coming up in March.

Chapter 28

Journey to Beautiful

Distant healing is taking place that we cannot observe or witness.

Life.

Perfect. Beautiful. Tender. Unpredictable. Precious. Fragile.

A gift of unknown time, unwrapped events to be opened at our choosing: moment by moment, breath by breath.

Inhale.

Inhale light. Inhale calm. Inhale sweet peace. Inhale this happy life.

All that I am. All that I stood for. All beautiful. All me

Exhale.

Exhale gratitude. Exhale melancholy recollections. Exhale joy-filled hopes. Exhale fulfilled wishes. Exhale this happy life.

Did I say, "I love you" enough? Did I tell you how special you were to me? Did I tell you how proud I am of you?

Did I?

Pain is lifting.

One hand waves goodbye as I blow my last kiss while the other reaches for home.

Floating weightless, I am zero degrees, I am content and comfortable, vast, and gloriously clear.

Wading in pure abundance.

I will send my spirit back to you.

I am the butterfly that catches your attention. I am the object represented by the moment I am in your thoughts, I am in your dreams,

You will recognize my fragrance. You will hear me laugh and see my smile. You will feel me as I warm your heart.

I am everything. I am everywhere. I surround you.

I was granted this gift of life. Now profoundly, passionately, I return by giving you the gift of my spirit. I place it gently, lovingly, peacefully in your heart.

And in yours. And in yours. And in yours.

Forever until we embrace again. Do not shed tears for my early departure. It is all in divine timing, and no actions would change this. I accept and walk toward it freely, learning all that I am.

Lover of life. Lover of family. Lover of friends. Lover of nature. Lover of generosity.

I am higher than I have ever been in purpose. Creatively and simplistically admiring the choices I've made. I received everything I ever needed, wanted, or longed for.

On the horizon I can see all that pulls me forward, all that I am and all that I am passionate about.

My heroes. My family. My friends. My pets. My life. My work.

My fight is over. Your battle begins.

Love and loss. Pain and joy. Tears and laughter. Guilt and hope. The insistent battle between head and heart. Allow your head to wave the white flag and surrender. Let your heart win victoriously.

I am peace. I am love. I am with you. I am forever. I am light. I am beautiful. I am your wife. I am your daughter. I am your friend. I am your sister. I am your confidant. I am many things to many people. I Am.

And I lived a journey to beautiful.

As I wrote in my journal on April 13, 2017 -One of my coworkers, thirty-five-year old Jessica, lost her battle with cancer today. Her passing inspired me to write the poem that appears as the entry for this chapter. Her father, Jeff, whom I also had the pleasure of working with, died eleven days ago. My thoughts were with their family, and I hoped they could embrace the collateral beauty in the order of their losses. I couldn't help but think that Jeff died before his daughter so that he could greet her on the other side.

Jeff, at the age of fifty-six and seemingly healthy, hadn't been feeling well, and within a very short amount of time, developed sepsis (a dangerous, life-threatening blood infection) and passed away.

Jeff's passing shocked everyone. According to his wishes, and in contrast to the typical gathering of mourners, he wanted a big party to celebrate his life. The owner where I work held a memorial in his honor, and it was there that I saw Jessica for the last time. She was so fragile but graciously accepted condolences while being pushed around the party-like atmosphere in her wheelchair. I hoped that she found joy in seeing how many people showed up to honor her dad's life and got the opportunity to possibly see her for the last time.

Just eight months later, I stood mournfully in front of a dear friend. My attention settled at his chest, where his hands had been placed perfectly in calm surrender. Hard-working hands that lay on top of where his heart should have been beating. How they so reminded me of my husband's hands. The same profession, the same loyalty, the same goals. Similar hands that matched a similar heart. A heart that loved a woman and a love that created two wonderful boys and made a family. The hands that fixed broken toys, bandaged skinned knees, and held his sons close to his heart. Hands that will forever guide his boys forward in their lives. A heart that embraced life, showed compassion, and cared for others. A heart that will forever be a guiding light for his family.

I stared at the forty-eight-year-old hands that looked so familiar. The years of integrity and grease so deeply embedded into the pores and calluses. A stained commitment that would eventually fade. I cried as I held my husband's hand and stared at the tired, sore hands that waved goodbye far too soon and left our hearts broken.

Saying goodbye to our dear friend Chuck felt so unfair. He had divorced several years ago, but found love and happiness again. Russ and I danced at his wedding just a few months ago. We missed his smile, his calm demeanor, and his "not a problem" attitude. I am sad for his family, for his boys, and his new bride. I am sad for my husband who lost his close friend. I can see the pain of loss in Russ's eyes, and that hurts my heart. In the time of deep mourning it was difficult to understand that this was Chuck's contract. It was in those moments I wondered why we must endure so much pain.

Teaching Moment: Loss is an inevitable part of our human experience. We experience loss in so many different ways. I can imagine the impact of the loss on these two families. While writing "Journey to Beautiful" I thought about my mom and my father-in-law and how different our relationships were. I thought about the different people they were. I wondered what they experienced in the days prior to their departure and what they experienced in the moments as they left the physical world. I thought about the loss of my mother and how it could have been different had we been able to heal our conflict. I thought about the events that led to the separation of my family and the choices I made to disconnect from what I felt was a toxic relationship. I thought of my own children and recognized how adult decisions rearranged their paths and interrupted their innocence. I thought about a conversation I had had with my nephew and niece, Adam and Allison, when my mom was dying. I shared my hurt, my bitterness, and my anger. We talked about unpopular choices their parents made and the choices my parents made and how similar they were. While recalling that conversation, I recognized the judgment that saturated so many conversations. I was in search of any audience that would have a sympathetic ear to my suffering. I needed anyone to agree with me and tell me I made the right decisions. Patterns emerged to show the similarities of the decisions my grandma, aunt, and mother made that took me away from my cousins . . . much the same way that my kids got taken away from their grandma, grandpa, cousins, family, and friends. The toxic patterns will continue if they are not realized, understood and healed out of existence. Loss has a way of bringing our life's choices to light and recognizing how those choices impact the people we love.

Chapter 29

More Jessicas

The morning after learning of Jessica's death, I was at the soul portion of my morning's well-being check-in, and the word "discernment" popped in. I was familiar with the word but not the definition. As is so often the case, I am surprised at how meaningful and significant these words are that come to me.

Encyclopedia.com defines discernment as, "The ability to judge well; perception in the absence of judgment with a view to obtaining spiritual direction and understanding; "Without providing for a time of healing and discernment, there will be no hope of living through this present moment without a shattering of our common life"; quality of being able to grasp and comprehend what is obscure; skill in discerning something; decide between truth and error."

I have looked at the things I've let go of that no longer nurture my future goals. I've looked at the things I have introduced into my life to propel me toward my future goals. I've eliminated the chorus that supported my old beliefs. I have vowed to choose love over fear. I choose joy over misery. I choose truth over falsity. I choose abundance over scarcity. I choose to remain curious and concentrate on the things that keep me learning. I choose to honor the contractual balance within. I embrace gratitude, peace, love, and calm.

During today's daily check-in, the word I heard for the *soul* portion was "innocuous." Again, I was unsure of the definition, and although it didn't resonate with me at the time, it sure made sense later in the day. Innocuous means "not harmful." Synonyms are "harmless," "safe," and "innocent." I liked safe because that was how my soul felt that day. It was May 31, 2017, Mom Abels's birthday, and she would have been ninety-four years old. It's hard for me to believe that she left the physical world thirty years ago.

Three things happened recently that I considered to be gifts for Russ and me from Mom Abels. The events began on Sunday. Russ and I were planting flowers, and while turning the corner near the rear of our house, we startled a baby robin. I spotted the mamma robin with her baby the day before and had watched the two of them make their way around the yard. I watched with a smile in my heart as the baby robin mimicked everything its mamma did. As we came around the corner, I could see what was going to happen, but I could not prevent it. Startled, the baby bird attempted to use its wings but stumbled right into our storm drain. Our storm drain is a cylinder about six inches in diameter and sticks out of the ground about eight inches and is buried about ten feet belowground. I stood over the storm drain and yelled to Russ, who was about fifteen paces ahead of me. He ran over and got down to try to help the baby bird out. We both made several attempts to rescue the poor baby bird, but we just couldn't reach it. Russ went inside to get a flashlight. We had lost sight of it, but we could hear it chirping. Mamma robin stayed close and kept looking in our direction as if she were asking for a status report. I am sure she knew her baby was in distress. We got a stick and tried to move the baby bird closer to the entry point. We tried other objects to attempt a rescue, but as soon as we got close, the frightened baby bird hopped away. It seemed the only way to free itself would be to walk the long, dark, cold length of the pipe that led out to the ditch on the north side of our property. I prayed that my guides, my animal angels would help this baby bird out of its scary predicament. We thought about pouring water down the pipe, hoping the force would push it to the end of the pipe, but I was too afraid we would drown the little robin. I wondered, *what's worse—trying to force it out with water and possibly drowning it, or the thought that it could starve to death down there?*

That night I dreamt that I saved the bird, only to wake up the next morning to the realization that I had not. I couldn't help but feel that it was our fault. It was an accident, but if we hadn't scared it, it wouldn't be trapped in that deep, dark hole. I struggle when animals are hurt, and I have a hard time letting the thoughts go. I tend to replay the events and allow it to upset me for quite a while. After about thirty hours of beating myself up, I found myself at yoga in the final pose of the evening. While there, I allowed myself to let go of the guilt. I reminded myself that we did nothing intentional to harm the creature, and it was out of my hands. Feeling terrible about the ordeal was not serving me or the baby bird. I prayed again for it not to suffer and pictured it walking toward the literal light at the end of the tunnel. I wore my mother-in-law's locket that day, the one that used to have a picture of my father-in-law in it. A piece of keepsake jewelry with a ruby stone on the outside and a picture of a handsome young soldier on the inside. The picture was lost years ago due to our overgrown puppy, Sprocket, and his adolescent behavior. He took the necklace off of my nightstand, and in his Lab-like determination to keep his treasures in his mouth, he fought me as I tried to retrieve it. The picture of the handsome soldier did not survive Sprocket's teeth or his saliva.

After the baby bird fiasco, I chose to wear my mother-in-law's locket to feel her close to me. The locket brought me comfort, and I wore it in honor of her birthday week. During my lunch break I started to read but couldn't stay focused, so I Googled, *How to help a baby bird that fell down a storm drain.* My search resulted in a lot of information to help a bird that fell out of its nest but not anything for one that was trapped underground. Then I decided to refine my search, (perhaps too wordy on my first attempt.) I Googled, *How long can a baby bird survive without its mamma, food or water?* The results were not promising. I started to imagine, for the baby robin's sake, that perhaps there was some water and maybe some bugs down in that tube. *Was it old enough to eat bugs?* I wondered.

Still determined to get a hopeful answer, I Googled, *fell down a storm drain,* and that search brought me to baby Jessica. I instantly remembered the story. An eighteen-month-old baby girl captured the hearts of America in 1987. Baby Jessica fell down her aunt's twenty-two-foot well in Texas. Her rescue and everything leading up to her rescue had been televised. The moment I saw that article appear in the search engine, I remembered Mom Abels sitting on her couch (yes, the brown one) watching that heart-wrenching story unfold. As the events surrounding baby Jessica's rescue evolved, I witnessed my mother-in-law's tormented heart and watched tears stream down her face. It was difficult watching Mom Abels so upset. In the eight years I had known her, I had never seen her that upset. It was a sad and scary story, but at that time I didn't have the experience as a mother to understand what she felt.

I couldn't help but feel the sweet synchronicity of the memory of my warmhearted mother-in-law. By searching the internet for my guilt-ridden heart to try to help a baby bird, I landed on a story that reminded me of an experience with my mother-in-law. An experience that, on her birthday, invited Mom Abels into my heart. She brought me a memory of when she felt helpless, just as I felt helpless. Her locket and her bright light were with me. She always understood me and made me feel better.

The following morning, while Russ and I were enjoying our coffee before getting ready for work, Russ noticed that our cat, Tom, had been acting strange. He was paying a lot of attention to things we could not see. He kept staring at the fireplace as if someone were there. He made several missed attempts to jump on top of the mantle. The mantle was covered with a collection of framed family photographs. I leaned over from my perch on the couch to entice Tom away from the mantle and was able to confirm that one of my treasured family pictures had indeed been disturbed. As I walked over toward Tom, who was still seated on the rocking chair in front of the mantle, I noticed that one of the pictures had fallen to the floor. It was lying facedown. When I leaned down and flipped it over, I discovered that it was the picture of Mom and Dad Abels dancing at our wedding. I laughed and put it back where it had been. It was odd and almost unexplainable that our cat could have gotten on top of the mantle and knocked over the middle picture in the back row without disturbing any other pictures.

I received a couple of acknowledgments from an honorable woman I got to call Mom. Yesterday, the Jessica story reminded me of her tender heart. It brought me back to our conversations and our special time spent together. And then, a cherished photo of my in-laws ended up on the floor. Unscathed and unbroken by its fall, they were both smiling at me as I returned the picture back to its place on the mantle.

I believe she was here, just to say hello, on her happy day.

Teaching Moment: There have been times while navigating and discovering my internal truths that I've felt so raw and bare-boned, stripped of everything I knew to be true. I experienced betrayals, gut-wrenching hurt, and painful realizations. It had been grueling and intense, and I was grateful for every second of it. My spiritual growth allowed me to acknowledge that while I was a different person in many ways, at the same time I was the same old me.

The tools I've developed to dig into my past have led me to a fundamental understanding with an ability to recognize my truths. My tools have introduced a self-discovery model that taught me how to allow a healthy reactive time in difficult experiences. At the same time, I've also learned to allow space to honor my humanness. I acknowledge through my struggles that it's okay to just be pissed off sometimes. It's ok to be sad, angry or mad too sometimes. I am the student, learning all I can to bring resolution within myself and to grow into the enormity of it all. Piece by piece, I'll allow the hurt and healing to shine warm rays of acceptance from the top of my head to the tips of my toes. My decision to be on this journey is overwhelming at times. It demands forward momentum. I cannot go back. To go back would be a betrayal of self.

There are so many layers of healing. As I peel back, as I go deeper and deeper; oftentimes it can feel as if I am descending. When I step back, as the observer, I am able to validate my growth. I am, indeed, ascending. I am allowing, understanding, and thriving while gaining peace and perspective. I must be fully engaged before I surface anew. I am ready to trust and surrender to uncertainty. I am ready to emerge into the person I was destined to be.

Part III-Surrender

Butterfly

A profound transformation has taken place, and I am aware of my personal metamorphosis. I am grateful for the people, places, and things that have been put on my path. Each has invited a continual deep introspection of where I have been and where I am encouraged to go.

I vow to make conscious decisions while walking this journey of the unknown. I've learned to trust and allow as each new mystery unravels in front of me. I have been guided through personal cycles of expansion and unlimited growth. I am a witness to the unveiling of the magic that is available in this abundant life. I have learned to go through life's changes with curiosity, grace, and light. I have watched my connection to material things fall away, providing space for my spiritual connection while I connect to my wisdom.

I am experiencing an unfolding. My mysteries and my gifts are exposing themselves to me. I am amazed at the limitless possibilities in all of these very unique parts of me—the parts that have been patiently waiting—and I am overjoyed at their arrival. I have been shown signs and symbols in my yoga practice, my dreams, my meditations, and my three-dimensional waking life. I am an active participant, mindfully paying attention and following the guided whispers from my spirit within and around me.

It is time to trust these wings and fly.

Chapter 30

Fishing and the Dance of the Butterflies

The strange commotion draws my attention. The sun shines brightly, and its reflection bounces off of the rocks. Sun-kissed bodies are warm and relaxed. I am surrounded by love. Generous family both around and out of the water. Fluttering wings captivate my attention. The colors magnetically draw my awareness to their message. I am being honored. I am being shown an abundance of life ever after. Love frees the roots deeply secured to the foundation below. Love sits carefully, steering our vessel toward shore. Love dances on the rock. The rock holds my past, present, and future.

When I made the conscious decision to embark on this spiritual journey, I chose my support team wisely. My experiences were becoming more and more bizarre, and I didn't share them with anyone for quite some time. I knew my tribe would continue to love and support me, but sharing felt vulnerable. I wasn't ready to expose the things I didn't understand myself. I did understand that I must trust the process and know that the people who would support me were already placed on my path. Knowing that truth was emotional gold!

The first vacation I took with Russ and his family was in 1983. Two years out of high school and well-ordained into his family for the better part of four years. I had not only fallen in love with Russ but I also loved his mom and dad. My very first Abels vacation was my introduction to fishing. It was also my first experience of being on a huge lake. We spent a week together at Russ's family's favorite vacation spot in Mountain Home, Arkansas.

Over the years we would repeat our annual trip, creating more wonderful memories. After Mom Abels's passing in 1987, just one year after Russ and I were married, our trips included Dad Abels, until his passing in 2001. Nick and Derrick never met their Grandma Abels but were blessed to have spent time and a couple of fishing trips with their papa.

We continued the Abels lake vacation tradition with our sons. Russ had enjoyed his favorite lake since he was a small boy, and I had spent the last thirty years falling in love with it too.

With each trip, as we'd get closer and closer to the lake, I would watch with anticipation as the landscape changed. The road would narrow, making it difficult for two vehicles to pass comfortably. I would clench my stomach as each vehicle approached in the opposite direction. The grade would increase, and again my stomach would clench as the boat we were pulling seemed to push us faster down the hills. The road would twist and curve, and then, I would get just a little peak. A break in the trees allowed just a quick glimpse of the tranquil, blue water. As soon as I would see it, I could smell it. Peace and calm would envelop my senses. "We are here," I'd announce to the boys.

It is an energy I cannot describe. The feeling of being at the lake inhabits every cell of my being. My shoulders release, and tension escapes my body. My inhales and exhales become slower and longer. I am calm. This is my peace. This is my joy and happiness. The lake is part of my family, and it feels like home.

We checked in at our favorite resort and pulled up to our cabin. As soon as we started unpacking, a pair of butterflies greeted us. I had never seen this type of butterfly before. Their wings were a vivid cobalt blue with a bold, black outline that broadened at the tips. This friendly duo were quite methodical as they flew around each of us. They fluttered up and down and around each one individually, as if they were checking us out. I got the distinct feeling that my in-laws were welcoming us back to our special place.

I saw the butterflies again when we parked near the dock. They flew around as we got our fishing gear out, and the pair escorted us all the way down to the boat. They continued to fly around us when we were on the boat, and they stayed with us until we left the no-wake area of the bay.

I noticed the butterflies every day. They greeted us each morning around the cabin and met us each evening when we returned to the dock. I greeted them with a silent hello, acknowledging their familiar presence.

During our first day on the water, I mentioned how much I loved the look of driftwood. Many of the residents near the lake, including the resort we stayed at, used driftwood in their landscaping. I liked the texture and the dimension the driftwood added in and around some of the homes we passed. That particular trip, the lake water was extremely low. The low water level had exposed all of the enticing driftwood treasures that had lain hidden beneath it for years.

Wednesday came and we had planned a full day of fishing. Each of us took a couple of rods and reels, making sure we had plenty of options to catch the big one. I noticed that Russ grabbed a hatchet out of the back of the truck (I didn't even know we had a hatchet in the back of the truck.)

I asked him why we needed a hatchet, and he said, "Never mind, you'll find out later."

I liked surprises and although I couldn't think of anything exciting that included the use of an axe, I knew Russ enjoyed surprising me, so I let it be. We fished for the first hour or so until the temperature began to climb and the fish were no longer hungry. We reeled in our lines and stowed away our rods. We trolled along the shoreline, enjoying the welcome breeze the movement provided.

I thought we were looking for a cooler cove to fish, but then Russ said, "Well, Mic, start looking for a piece of driftwood that you like."

I looked at Russ and both boys, and it dawned on me, *that's why you brought the axe.*

"Really?"

Russ nodded yes, and we trolled along the shore shopping for a unique Norfork Lake treasure. As we came to one of our favorite bluffs, I spotted a perfect piece of driftwood that looked like a picture to me.

I pointed to it, and Russ asked, "The one all the way at the top of the ridge?"

I responded excitedly, "Yep. Sorry!"

Nick and Derrick jumped in the water, and Russ handed them the axe. They swam to shore ready to cut away our very own piece of our favorite place. I was so excited and also touched that my husband and boys had planned this for me. As my sons jumped in the lake I thought, *they will do well to mimic their dad's romantic gestures with their future wives.*

"Will we have enough room in the boat for that? And what about in the truck on the way home?"

R uss said, "Don't worry about it, we'll make room."

Nick and Derrick swam to shore, climbed up the rocks, found the driftwood I had my eye on, and started swinging the axe. They chopped away at the base. Soon, the dead tree was free from its anchor, and the boys gave the thumbs-up that they had accomplished the task at hand.

As we approached the shore, I noticed a commotion on a flat rock just in front of the boat. My attention was no longer on Russ or the boat or on the boys or the driftwood. There was so much activity, I could not take my eyes off of the rock. As the boat moved closer, I was able to get a clearer view of what was in front of me.

The surface of the rock was covered in what I guessed to be more than one hundred butterflies. There were so many that the rock appeared to be moving. Each one was an exact replica of the two that had been following us all week. In a frenzy of activity, they fluttered around and created a mesmerizing kaleidoscope of blue and black. As we floated closer, I was overwhelmed by their beauty. I had never witnessed so many butterflies in one place. I scrambled for my camera. I wanted to capture the unbelievable sight. I fumbled around but I couldn't get my camera to work. I was torn. I wanted a picture to freeze the moment in time, but I didn't want to stop looking and miss any of it. I was able to take one picture before my camera fell out of my hands. I started to lean over to pick it up when I heard the instructions, *Just watch. Take it all in.*

I stared and wondered. *Why were they here? What's so special about that rock? What brought them all here at once?* And then I heard a whisper, *"We are all here. We are all here for you."*

Without time to organize or make sense of what was happening, I could only trust my instinct. My immediate overall feeling was that of family. As I gazed at the breathtaking scene, my intuition told me that each family member's spirit was represented as a butterfly on the rock. Although I wanted to capture that fascinating moment on film, I suddenly realized that I was not meant to record the experience digitally, I was to experience it spiritually. It was a private message meant for me, to notice it and breathe deep into my heart. In those few moments of unexplainable love, I stopped to breathe it in and to allow the magic to wash over me. As each butterfly flew away, I acknowledged their presence and thanked each one for their visit. I felt pure bliss as an overwhelming feeling of love and support blanketed me.

That was the first time an experience with spirit moved me to such depths. In that moment, I felt everything was as it should be. I felt understood. I felt supported and guided. I was grateful to have the awareness to recognize and acknowledge the symbolism of spirit and witness its profound and magnificent dance!

Chapter 31

Just Write

When I started a journal to record my thoughts and experiences, it became a reminder of how much I liked writing and how much I loved words. Words are powerful. I learned several years ago just how much I loved words and storytelling through journaling. I was introduced to the practice of journaling in the scrapbooking community. I became interested in scrapbooking because I had always loved pictures. When I held a photograph in my hand, I felt each picture had a story that begged to be told. I wanted to know the people and the places and all of the intricate details captured in a moment in time. I felt a connection and almost a responsibility to tell the stories that were woven within each of the images. I spent countless hours (and money, which my husband will attest to) creating scrapbook pages and allowing my creativity to flow as I designed each page. Soon, I found myself getting less and less focused on the layout and design of the page as my passion turned to the importance of recording the story onto the scrapbook page. It became primal for me to leave a legacy for my family. To offer a little part of me that they could hold in their hands and know what my heart was feeling at the exact moment the shutter clicked.

I have entered the fall season of my life, the sixth decade. So many changes have settled within me. As I explore the vibrant, warm colors of my life thus far, time has allowed me to look back with clarity and gratitude. I continue to satisfy my spiritual hunger. I am trying to understand my life's experiences, feeding my soul again and again and again.

I began to question whether or not what I wrote was worth sharing. I asked for guidance from trusted friends and family. Should I start a blog? Would my guidance and practices that I've adopted help others? Was my manuscript worthy of being a tool for teaching? From my research, if I were to take my writing seriously, I would need to build a platform and an audience. I never had an account on social media. I would have to change my previously narrow opinions about social media and broaden my online presence. That meant I would have to learn how to build a website, set up social media accounts, post content, and keep up with all of it. Thinking about all of that caused me some serious anxiety. I needed to release the hold the anxiety had on me. I needed to share so I could release it.

I shared my anxiety about all of these topics with Russ. I outlined different ideas I had and told him that I was not sure what to do. After listening and hearing everything I had to say, Russ looked at me with his always confident and supportive eyes and said, "Just write, Mic, just keep on writing."

That simple answer paired with his unwavering belief in me was all I needed. Russ has always been able to calm my nerves by simplifying the impossible and quieting my anxious mind. He supports my ideas, no matter how crazy they feel or sound. Russ is my rock, my support, my cheerleader, and my forever love.

I settled my head onto my pillow that night with a renewed sense of confidence.

The following morning was Sunday. I poured myself a cup of coffee and stood at the windows in the sunroom, staring out at the flutter of activity just beyond the glass. I wrapped both hands around my favorite extra-large coffee mug. As the heat from my morning beverage warmed my hands, I brought it to rest just under my nose.

I closed my eyes and allowed the caffeine-induced aroma to tease my sleepy taste buds. Waking up my senses reminded me of what I went to bed thinking about the night before. I took my first sip and thought of how I should use my experiences to help others. Just as that thought entered my mind, three huge crows landed on the ground just feet in front of me. They stared at me and cocked their heads inquisitively. The crows were a significant sign for me. I read somewhere that crows are an omen of change and are able to see past, present, and future simultaneously. They are representations of creation and spiritual strength. They unite both the light and the dark and should be held with utmost respect.

After seeing the crows, I remembered that I woke up in the wee morning hours. The alarm clock that reflects the time onto the ceiling on my husband's nightstand read 3:33 a.m. I had been seeing the numbers 333 for the past few days. Because I am compelled to learn as much as I can about signs and symbols and their meanings, I did the research. My findings verified that seeing 333 is spiritual and significant. The Universe was sending energy my way. This is positive, creative energy and involves encouragement, communication, freedom, and assistance. It may also signify the presence of the ascended masters. These are spiritual healers, teachers, and prophets who guide us from the spirit realm. When you are in a life situation where you need encouragement, the ascended masters will use the number 333 to signal their appearance in your life. I know that at the heart, at the base, at my foundation, it is imperative that I open up, pay attention, and acknowledge the signs and symbols that I have seen and felt and understand the experience on all levels.

Teaching Moment: Remain curious and aware. Always pay attention, and when you feel as though an answer or validation has come to you in the form of symbolism, believe it. You would not feel compelled to see the synchronicity in the symbolism unless there was a message in it for you. I had been feeling anxious as to how to move forward with my ideas of writing and sharing. Russ calmed my nerves, which allowed space to become creative. This space also allowed for signs of validation. Three crows and seeing the numbers 333 made me pause. The pause invited some research. The research offered validation about my future and my emotions about the future I wanted to design for myself. When that internal nudge is present, follow the path that leads to what feels right in your

heart. Trust in your genius and surrender to your internal knowing.

Chapter 32

Are You Listening?

I hear the train whistle in the distance, softly muffled by the dense fog that blankets the landscape. Curious, I barter for a ticket, not knowing the destination. Shall I choose first-class? Coach? Does it matter? The cars glide along recognizable and unrecognizable scenery. Some are known to me and feel familiar. Others are new and unfamiliar. Some dark, some luminous. The sun comes up, the rooster crows. Every twenty-four hours we get a brand-new day of choices.

Am I the passenger or the conductor?

Validation comes in all forms. I vow to stay present and tune in and be open to the messages. This journey comes with its fair share of unrelenting doubts and uplifting validations.

I saw my mom's look-alike in the health food store as I shopped. Seeing her gave me chills, and my stomach sank. The moment I acknowledged the woman's resemblance to my mother, I had an overwhelming feeling of a much-needed reinforcement. *You are not alone.* Yesterday I kept thinking, *I have no one to go to, I have to do this all by myself.* Even though I have support from family and friends, I was feeling overwhelmed by committing to the idea of writing. My feelings of overwhelm led to feeling alone. Following my passion to write and share it publicly began to make me feel exposed and vulnerable. I marinated in this head battle for a good portion of the day. But today, much to my surprise, my mom validated that I am not alone. I was so grateful for her message. The feeling made tears well up as I allowed myself to feel the intensity of her peaceful communication.

When I returned to my vehicle in the health food store parking lot, I had a brief moment of visual pain. I am not sure how else to describe it. It was a vision, a waking dream, for lack of a better term. In it, I was a little girl. My ponytail was swaying side to side as I skipped along, holding a balloon. Suddenly, I stumbled and fell. I looked at my balloon. It was deflated, limp, and lifeless on the ground beside me.

That vision felt symbolic of how I felt about writing publicly: deflated, fallen, and skin-kneed. I was happy and excited one moment, and the next moment I tripped over something I didn't see in front of me. And in an instant my outlook, my mood, had changed.

I struggled with the uncertainty of what I was being shown. This piqued my awareness, and I continued to be distracted as my attention was on everything that was happening to me in both my waking and sleeping world. I experienced a waking dream when I saw my mom's look-alike, which made me recall my sleeping dream the night before.

In that dream, a little girl showed up at my door, crying. I asked, "Who are you, and where do you need to be?" The little girl did not speak but handed me a school folder. The folder had scribbled writing that looked like the letters "A," two "N's," and another "A." It appeared to spell out *Anna*. During the dream, I kept waking up and falling back asleep. Each time I drifted back to sleep, I continued my dream. Each time that happened, the little girl got younger and younger until she was a baby. At the point when the little girl became an infant, I was in a panic to try to find out where she belonged.

When I woke up, the first thing I thought about was the name in my dream. As I pictured the name Anna, I realized it was a palindrome, a word spelled the same backward and forward. I believed that symbolized my journey back to self. A return to the beginning of where I began.

In my dream analysis research, I learned that it's important to pay attention to both the detail in dreams and the overall emotional feeling of the dream. My question to the little girl in the dream was not, "*Where do you live?*" but rather, "*Where do you need to be?*" I felt this represented my quest for direction.

The overall panic I felt in my dream represented not knowing where I belong yet. I have felt unsure of where I fit in. The emotion, the overall feeling in my dream, represented my inner struggle with the outward acceptance of my newly uncovered beliefs. The dream was symbolic of my waking life. I am trying to navigate which path to follow and which life is mine.

Teaching Moment: The decision to write publicly held a huge responsibility for me. Sharing publicly meant that my struggles and my spiritual experiences would no longer be private. I am selective when it comes to the people I choose to share my life with. I share with friends and family who have proven I can trust their confidence. When somebody I care about trusts me with their personal experiences, I assume they've shared in confidence. Out of mutual respect, I would expect the same from them. By sharing my experiences publicly, my intention is to help anyone going through a similar experience. My hope is to offer guidance for healing. I am in a battle between honoring an old belief of family secrets, which is just another word for shame, and exposing my beliefs and experiences to help others. If I am totally honest, fear of judgment is front and center right now. Keeping all of this to myself is safe. Keeping all of this to myself is familiar. Sharing my stories feels brave. The result of sharing my stories is unknown. The unknown is terrifying but has also proved to be invigorating. The scales tip toward the unknown. Scary but exciting. New and unfamiliar. My heart is guiding me toward the edge. When I close my eyes and envision my future, I am grateful for taking the risk.

Chapter 33

White Gloves and Dinners at 9

Russ and I have always been conscientious about the cleanliness of our home. We were both taught, from an early age, that cleanliness and order reflect the responsibilities of owning a home and also shows respect for the things you work hard to obtain. When I started working a so-called normal nine-to-five job, cleaning day was Saturday. Russ has worked Saturdays for years. It pleased me to know that it pleased Russ to come home to a nice, clean house after a long workweek.

On one particular Saturday afternoon, as Russ came in from a long day at work, he announced that the top of the refrigerator needed to be cleaned. I was tired; I had cleaned all day. I followed the cleaning ritual, as I did every Saturday, with the grocery shopping ritual. I had just sat down and gotten up to greet him at the door, only to hear his disapproval. His comment irked me, to say the least. Typically, I would have become defensive and my head voice, in all of its pent-up anger, would have fought back. *Well, if you don't like it, why don't you clean it?* But I wouldn't have stopped there. I would have allowed the comment to fester and marinate for another second, and my inner dialogue, my negative head chatter would have continued.

I gave up my entire Saturday so you could come home to a clean house. You don't ever say anything nice about the rest of the house, and you only point out what I didn't do. God, I swear, what if I never cleaned anything? Why can't you just appreciate what I do every day? I make your dinner, I clean your clothes and I put them away like you're a goddamned two-year-old child . . . And on and on it would go.

He made a comment. I ordinarily would not have cared what his intention was, I would have already decided that I needed to get as defensive as possible. I would have defended my feelings based on the "how dare you say anything negative about me" attitude. First, I want to clarify an untruth. My husband does, in fact, notice and comment on how great the house looks when he gets home every Saturday, without fail. To review, this is my rant. My ego had been triggered. To defend my ego, I was prepared to bring everything and anything into the argument for always and all time. I might embellish my story to support my defensiveness. My defensive ego was not going to listen to logic. I was triggered, and I was ready to fight. I held all of this in, getting myself more and more agitated and ready to lash out. *Just try it, you are walking on eggshells here . . . just say something else, I dare you,* continued my overly irritated head voice.

But this Saturday was different. The work I've done, the tools I've developed allowed me to navigate this differently. I first acknowledged that Russ was not my enemy. We are on the same team. He felt a need to point out a cleaning omission for some unknown reason. A reason that I have never even attempted to ask about because I am too busy defending my wounds. But on that particular day, instead of diving into the defensive, self-deprecating, how-dare-you familiar rhetoric, I simply responded by saying, "Okay, yeah I'll get to that later."

He simply replied, "Okay."

I had engaged my "mindful thought redirection" practice. No fight. No internal battle. But, for me, it couldn't end there because my work had just begun. I had to ask myself why his comment made me want to scream and yell and get so reactive. So I began the work. I ignored the negative ego ions (the head chatter defending my old wounds) and got my tools out and started digging.

I started by thinking back to all the negative comments about my cleaning. I started to think about my experiences at home and how much fun we had cleaning the house, listening to music and, of course, getting the sweet reward of TV and an allowance. I dug even deeper, trying to recall negative comments. Nothing came up right away, so I continued, trying to recall an earlier wound.

I had a quick glimpse of me at approximately nine years of age. I was in the bathroom scrubbing the sink and crying. *Oh yeah, I remember that. Why did that happen? Why was I crying and cleaning?* I closed my eyes to invite a clear memory. I rewound the story to recall the details that had led up to that event. I remembered. I awoke late at night to my mom and dad fighting. My mom was crying and begging my dad to stop yelling. The next thing I remembered was that I was in my pajamas, crying, and recleaning the bathroom, which had been my responsibility that night. I don't remember anything else that happened that night. I remembered that

I felt bad for my mom. Maybe I voluntarily started cleaning because I felt bad that my mom was getting yelled at. Or maybe my dad woke me up and made me reclean the bathroom and that upset my mom. I am not clear on how I arrived back in the bathroom to clean it again, but I do know what the experience felt like.

I was the little ponytailed girl, holding the balloon, and I tripped over something I didn't see in front of me. I was crying and scrubbing, attempting to fix it. My responsibility that night for cleaning the bathroom did not pass my father's inspection. The job I did wasn't good enough. I upset my mom and my dad. After allowing myself to recall and feel the memory, the wound from that event that I had buried so deep inside wasn't just that the job wasn't good enough—*I wasn't good enough.*

I began to cry as I recalled the event. I cried for my nine-year-old self. I cried for the sweet, sensitive little girl who was changed by her experience. I cried for my adult self and all the years I didn't care about myself. I cried for all the stupid arguments I had allowed because I didn't understand. I cried for loving myself enough to try to figure my shit out.

Using focus and awareness, I was able to understand where the wound originated. By recalling the experience, it explained why I was so defensive about my husband's *clean* comment. I granted myself the space to consider something bigger at work. I found a huge opening of understanding for myself. I found the ability to visit an impactful experience I had had as a young girl and realize years later that I was continuing to react to it. My tools and the work revealed the event that led to *why* I had built a wall to protect my wounded child. And how that resulted in such a negative, reactive response from me when she, the younger version of myself, and the wound needed defending. I was able to detach my husband from the comment and not react defensively toward him. Because I responded to Russ's comment instead of reacting, I met his needs, which allowed time for me to discover a vital part of me. My husband had some stuff to deal with in his past that allowed a dusty refrigerator top to bother him enough to say something, but that is *his* to work through. I was able to separate ownership. I had the knowledge and did the work to uncover an answer that helped me understand and heal.

Growth allowed a healthy response that respected me and my husband. Proof of my positive transformation.

During Nick and Derrick's high school years, as their lives became busy with sports and social activities, our dinner times experienced a huge shift. Since the boys were very young, we were bound by a routine that included a schedule for dinner, homework, and showers. Russ and I agreed that it was important to sit down at the table and have dinner together as a family. This precious time provided moments for us to connect and share what was going on in our individual daily lives.

I would like to blame basketball in particular for the big shift in our dinner routine, being the longest season, not only in months but also the length of each individual game. Depending on their year in high school, I cheered the boys on for two games in a row—junior varsity and varsity. Away games left even less time between dinner and bedtime. After a game we would find a place to eat on our way home. Depending on the time of night and how far we were from home, we would either stop and eat with friends or hit a fast-food drive-through and eat as we drove home. Because I would get home too late to make dinner for Russ, we would bring dinner home, and Russ would end up eating closer to 10 p.m.

As our lives changed, so did our routines. Over time, on non-sports nights the boys and I would eat closer to 7:30 or 8:00 p.m., and Russ would choose to eat later as he was usually busy with one project or another. This started to be a habit, and before we knew it, the kids were out of the house but Russ continued to eat at 9 p.m. His choice aggravated me to no end. I allowed this to give me a huge amount of turmoil. I made several attempts to change what I believed was an unhealthy habit. I stuck to my guns and explained that it was not good to eat so late and go to bed on a full stomach. Everything I read supported my disapproval of his chosen dinnertime.

I, of course, ate at a *normal* dinnertime. But, normal was getting closer and closer to 8 p.m. for me. Because of my upbringing and doting on my dad, and since the day Russ and I were married, I continued to serve or at least plate his dinner. Oftentimes that moved the kitchen cleanup closer to 10 p.m. I had been getting up at 4 a.m. to allow an hour of meditation each morning, so by 9 p.m. I was finding it difficult to keep my eyes open.

Each night I got more and more agitated about dinner and the time involved in the cleanup afterward. I felt it was a huge disrespect for my time, which made me crabby. I created an emotional downward spiral that would lead to a huge blowup. I kept everything in the volcano until it had no choice but to erupt into an overflowing, emotionally charged pissing match.

Indeed, the blowup occurred, and it became clear that I was not going to win the pissing match, or change my husband or his preferred dinnertime.

Once again, I needed to look at how *I* could change or at least change my reaction to the stubborn man I had married. Or try to determine why his resolve bothered me so much or why his dinnertime bothered me so much.

I knew I had created the monster—after all, I was the one who started and continued to dote on my husband, and that was not his fault. *When had my wanting to please him change into an annoyance that made me bitter?*

It was time to start digging. Time to get the toolbox out and begin the work.

I asked myself a number of questions. *Why does this bother me so much? When did his controlling behavior begin to piss me off? Is it the dinner hour or the controlling that is the issue?* I spent a decent amount of time peeling back the layers of my life's events, trying to determine when I had felt similar feelings of disrespect for my time. Or feelings of being controlled or a general annoyance of being expected to perform.

I was unable to recall a single event but I did recall a block of time back in the early '80s when my parents were operating their leather business. There was a span of time when I arrived home before my sisters or my parents, and I voluntarily made dinner. I remembered that I didn't mind making dinner, and I had chosen to do so. I remembered, however, that when my mom would ask me to make dinner or would make comments about it being easier on her if I made dinner, I would get highly agitated. If making dinner was my idea, I was fine with it. I was more than fine with it because the intention was to surprise my folks, knowing they would have one less thing to do. As soon as my intention of helping was taken away, it became a chore, a responsibility, an expected duty. To me, asking turned to expecting, and expecting took away the appreciation.

By digging up this memory, I remembered a familiar defiant attitudes. *How dare you. Why was this a problem? I couldn't be told what to do? Was I that rebellious? Did I not feel appreciated? Was I not noticed or seen? Did I need attention, or was I that controlling?* I was aware that I had issues with not being seen. I could validate the feelings of wanting attention, appreciation, and approval, but I never thought of myself as controlling. *Me? Oh my God, it is me!* My jaw could have hit the floor.

I had allowed myself to be consumed with my opinion of the dinner issue. I had pointed fingers of blame and accused my husband of being controlling. And maybe he was, but my discovery was quite a revelation for me. It proved that I also suffered from the same malady.

After I discovered that little gem, I wanted to understand how to change my reaction to the dinnertime debate. I continued the work and asked myself, *What would be gained by winning this argument? What was my endgame? How would I feel if tomorrow I didn't have Russ in my life? What if it was only me, and I could cook whenever I wanted and eat whenever I wanted? What if?* Those thoughts felt drastic, but the reality of the situation was that it came down to choosing my battles. How would I feel if I was victorious after bitching long enough to get my own way? What if tomorrow my battle was over and I could eat all alone at whatever time I wanted for the rest of my life?

I granted myself permission to let go of attempting to control this issue. It could no longer be a battle for me. I stood at the stove, crying over the thought of losing my husband. I cried over the thought of how petty my self-induced time restraints had been. I promised myself, at the moment of clarity, to let go of my ridiculous control. A control I had been feeding because of an old, unhealed wound that stemmed from what felt like a lack of appreciation.

I was well aware that I lacked self-confidence. Back then and now, I remembered reading that a lack of self-confidence could lead to control issues. One of the most difficult parts of embarking on my spiritual journey, doing the work, and consciously becoming aware of self was discovering some unbecoming truths about myself. The truths that held negative connotations were the hardest to accept. It was important to understand my behavior in an attempt to change for the better. Understanding why I behaved the way I did not only allowed space for me, but it also allowed me to grant precious space for others.

Teaching Moment: See yourself in your circumstances as the observer. The result of the work on these two events led to my discovery that we all have ownership in what we say and how it is received. Intention is represented in our actions. Words are powerful. I know my husband would walk through fire for me. He does not say or do things to intentionally upset me. My unhealed wounds are what trigger the emotional backlash. Are there things he says that upset me? Absolutely. But if I consider he has good intentions, I am less likely to have a reaction based on my defensive impulses in an effort to defend my ego. Both of these lessons proved to teach me some hard truths about myself. I was able to recognize similar emotions of lack. Lack was disguised as not feeling good enough and not being appreciated. It is important to drill down and recognize when you believed something about yourself that was based on someone else's opinion of you or your actions. The truth is we don't know what to do with these emotions as young people. We know that it didn't feel good. We acknowledge that we don't want to feel like that again, so we stuff the emotion down, cover it up, and defend the wound at all costs. All of this goes on subconsciously. We don't think about why we are reacting, we know we are hurt or in pain or triggered. By recalling and understanding the initial or equally emotional event, you can begin the work of dismantling the walls of defensiveness. The reason acknowledging the origin of your wound is vital in healing is that it lessens your reactive period. You can make it a practice to be mindful of your reactive period by becoming aware of your wounds. By becoming aware, the healing process has begun. Healing happens when we pay attention to our needs and, as the observer, gently navigate our role in any given event, past or present. We are human and we have emotions, so we will continue to be triggered. If you are familiar with your wounds and you have started the healing process, you will be well-equipped to catch yourself when reactive. You are human, you will react. The key is to not stay in a reactive period long enough to activate the hormones of stress. Stress, over time, has a negative physical and emotional effect on our bodies, minds, and spirits.

I must continue to be open and honest if I desire a healthy change for growth and self-love in my life. Doing the work, using the tools to dig takes deep introspection and harsh honesty. You are

a mystery, and so is everyone in your life. Become a supreme

observer of you, your life, and everyone around you, and the

mystery becomes a treasure to behold.

Chapter 34

Geese, Gratitude, and a Healing Visit

A frozen February morning leaves winter scents on the exposed blades of grass. My four-legged companion, Izzy, is sniffing every inch of the frozen ground. Her full winter coat keeps her safe while enjoying the cold and snow. She rolls around on her back, jumps up and dives, nose first into a pile of snow. She lives in the present moment. She is teaching me to do the same. A welcomed flock of geese fly and honk overhead. I believe they know how important they are to me. Personal symbols of light, acknowledgment, and validation. I've adopted winged creatures as representatives of three special spirits.

Mom, Mom Abels, and Dad Abels.

Hello & good morning.

It's early, but today feels balanced. I have been experiencing more and more days that feel like this. Days that came after countless hours of soul-searching and drilling down for self-discovery. I've felt closer to whole than I have in a long time. Not every day feels like this. Some days, I return to the old familiar self. The improved, in balance days are falling closer and closer together. A deliberate and determined *me* dug down to recognize the old wounds so I could heal them one by one. I vow to continue the promise to myself. Healing helps me achieve balance and feel gratitude for everything in my life. My gratitude shines so bright, it illuminates deep within my heart and opens limitless possibilities.

Gratitude allowed deep comfort within my mind, body, and soul. I set daily intentions to be in constant gratitude and try to see love in everything around me. Giving love and receiving love with a whole heart keeps me in a healthy mindset.

A few good months had passed, and I stood outside under the overcast April sky. I felt such joy. The spring rain offered a spiritual rinse in nature and in me. I placed my palms together and raised them overhead. I gazed toward the sky, expressing gratitude. As the rain fell upon my eyelids, I heard a couple of geese honking. I opened my eyes, but I could not see them. *They must be just above the clouds*, I thought. They honked again and appeared in the cloud break, confirming there were two of them. A smile spread across my face—acknowledgment, validation, and thoughts confirmed. So much to be grateful for today.

I attended yoga classes on a regular basis, four to five times per week. Yoga is a mindful practice for me, but I often struggled with letting go of my day. As I tried to calm my mind for this particular Monday evening class, I found it difficult to pay attention.

Amy, my yoga teacher, greeted her class and offered a quick introduction before we began. Within ten minutes, while focusing on deep breaths, I was able to let the thoughts go, and I was plugged into Amy's challenging flow.

At the end of class, while expressing gratitude for my practice and for showing up to give myself an hour of personal care, I noticed my head started to pull to the right and up, as it often does during meditation. I thought it was odd that it was happening while I was lying down. As the cool, refreshing, lemon lavender cloth was placed on my forehead, I guided my head to the center once again. We were invited to roll onto our right side and come to a sitting position. With my hands in prayer at heart center, I bowed forward while speaking a salutation, *Namaste*. I used the scented, cool towel to wipe my arms and the back of my neck. I brought it to my face and wiped my forehead and cheeks. I brought it under my nose and held it there so I could inhale the luxurious scent deep into my lungs. The soothing aroma infused my already very relaxed and grateful state. I started to think about the head pulling. It had never happened in yoga before.

The first time I experienced head pulling was in a group meditation class. Although, during the meditation, I was unaware of it. When the meditation was over and I arrived back in my body and opened my eyes, I realized my head was facing up and to the far right. At first, it made me curious. It was beginning to happen in all my meditations, and I was starting to become aware of it. As soon as I would relax, the head pulling would begin. I researched to see if there was something symbolic in this almost uncontrollable pull I had been experiencing. I didn't find anything that seemed to be relevant in meditation or in yoga, but it was beginning to bother me.

The following evening, I attended Ashley's yoga class. I have had many emotional experiences in Ashley's class, and I believe it is because I feel safe in her lighthearted, nurturing, peaceful space. The subject of emotional release had come up several times in each of my yoga classes. It's beneficial to know so students are aware that it can be a part of a yoga experience. I was fine during the entire class. My practice felt good, and I was pleased with the energy. While on my mat, lying in final *savasana*, I noticed the same head pulling. My head started to pull to the right just as it had the night before. *Why is this happening?* I wondered. I pulled my head back to center, but it felt as if there was a resistance. It felt as though I were pulling against a magnetic force.

At the moment of feeling the magnetic energy, I felt my mother's presence. I could feel her cradling both sides of my face and along the bottom of my jaw, with her hands. As soon as I felt her cradle my head with her hands, she began guiding it back to the right and upward. Her face was right under my lower right jaw, almost nestled in my shoulder. As soon as I acknowledged her presence, I saw her smile. It was the same smile she had given me in the hospital after her stroke. The smile that said, *I'm so glad you're here.*

To experience her touch and see her smile and know she was so close was such a sweet, simple, moving, profound experience. Tears began to well up. They fell down my cheeks and landed on my yoga mat beneath me. Soon, I began sobbing, as the feelings of love and hope overwhelmed my senses. I silently expressed gratitude for my mother and thanked my mom for her significant visit.

Teaching Moment: Yoga is a moving meditation. It offers an introduction to travel within. Yoga has not only strengthened my spirit but it has also supported my journey to learn more about my soul. It offers peace for sixty minutes while I ask my body to twist and balance and stand like a warrior. I've read about how each pose, or *asana*, is directly connected to help facilitate harmony in our bodies. Yoga invited me to learn about the seven main energy centers in my body and learn of their importance concerning emotional blockages. I am so very blessed to have the smart, educated, and caring yoga teachers in my life. Through their example, I feel a yearning to learn all I can and embrace the knowledge that yoga brings to my life. Yoga has taught me to focus solely on my breath and to trust in that breath to get me through physical and emotional discomfort. Our breath is one of the most important tools we have to initiate calm. Yoga offered a safe space for me to quiet my mind long enough to connect to higher realms of

consciousness. The stillness has opened the portals that allow me to

connect to things truly divine.

Chapter 35

Magic Messages

Hidden strands of silk intricately woven into a unique tapestry become visible upon first light. The sun glistens off the heavy dew, weighing down each of the threadlike walls. Brisk Indian summer temperatures invite a glorious palette of color. I breathe in the cool, damp air. Feeling it enter my nostrils, inviting it to travel down the back of my throat and move slowly through my esophagus, as it fills my lungs. Oxygen spreads across my back, around into my abdomen as it delivers warmth, peace, and calm. I surrender while gazing at this wondrous miracle of nature. A spider suspends itself magically off center. I want to stay here forever. I want to stay suspended in this magic forever.

Russ and I had an open and meaningful conversation. I feel such a deep connective energy of our love when we share on a soulful level. We covered many topics during our conversation, but one of the things we discussed was the psychic reading I had witnessed the night before. I was part of a group reading given by Missy, a medium who lives in our area. There were about twenty people present. I was so moved by her gift that I decided I would like my own personal reading from her. Russ believes that I already know what I need to know and questioned why I felt I needed a psychic reading. I explained that I felt as if there were some loose ends concerning my relationship with my mom. I believe that we get the healing messages we need, and I was ready to hear what I needed. Russ has always supported me in whatever it was I felt I needed to do. With his support, I was excited to call Missy and make an appointment.

I was at a place in my journey where I felt a reading with Missy would be very beneficial to my healing work. Through my process, there have been feelings of anger, hurt, and betrayal. I felt a need to connect with my mom, and I wanted to hear from Mom and Dad Abels too. There were many loved ones I wanted to hear from, but I was yearning to hear my mother's words. I felt she woud be able to speak to me from a different perspective than when she was in the physical world.

The following is my reading with Missy, the medium. My Uncle Dave and my cousin Todd came through first.

"Uncle is an absolute mess. Mind isn't right around his death, heart area, long-standing illness; legs don't feel right, and the medication messes with his head. He is grumpy."

I share that I didn't know that much about his last days. We grew apart in geographical distance but also in emotional distance. I was reminded of his comments to me in the hospital when he came to visit my mom. He took me aside in the hospital hallway and hinted that I needed to "Fix this, life is too short." I was pissed that he thought I was the one who needed to fix it. He must not have been aware of any of the *fixing* I had already tried to do, so I smiled passively and let him state his peace. Looking back, it was good advice, considering he knew his sister pretty well. He probably figured she wasn't going to be the one doing any of the fixing.

Missy continued, *"Your uncle is still attached to life, very attached to you, and loved living life."*

I always felt close to Uncle Dave. We had a good relationship. He made me laugh, and he was the fun uncle. He wouldn't care if you got in trouble, mostly because he would be the one instigating it. It had been so long since his son Todd's death, I hadn't thought of him in years. Todd's death was never talked about. Todd was very young when he drowned, and I am sure the pain kept everyone quiet about it. I was glad to hear that Todd and Uncle Dave were together. Missy explained that the recently departed struggle and stay attached to earthly stuff.

She continued, *"There is a strong connection between your uncle and your dad. Your uncle or your dad are very lucky in life, right place, right time, everything falls into place. He also says the reading, this medium stuff is a bunch of bullshit but is interested that it is happening. He feels his funeral was over the top. Much bigger than expected. Too much money involved."*

Mom Abels was the next one to come through. Missy said, *"She is a sweet soul. She had a long illness."*

I shared that she suffered from Parkinson's disease for a long time. Missy shared that Mom Abels showed Christmas tree ornaments.

"She appreciated the tree you decorated with all of their ornaments."

I called it the retro tree. I used my in-law's tree, lights, ornaments, and tree topper. When I decided to use all of their Christmas decorations, it was to both honor them and fill the house with the wonderful memories of the past. I couldn't believe that after fifteen years, all of the tree lights still worked! Mom Abels added, *"There hasn't been much to celebrate in the past couple of years, but this one you will be able to enjoy."*

Missy asked if she had a daughter.

Missy told me, *"She says she views you as a daughter. She looks out for you too!"*

Missy was shown a guardian angel pin by Mom Abels and Missy explained that our guardian angels are our protectors in the physical world. Missy was busy listening and jotting down notes as she was being shown things or made to feel things. She said she is not sure if the reference to the pin means I have an angel pin or if this is a metaphor. She concluded with Mom Abels by stating, *"She is moving freely on the other side and feels good."*

Dad Abels was next to come through.

"He's easygoing, there is a lightness to him. He is a bit of a stinker, an ornery booger. He would do stuff and play stupid about it. Like kid guilty, got caught with his hand in the cookie jar. He hurts. His back hurts. There's concern over care. The medication messed with his head; he feels out of it. He was absolutely greeted by people before he went. He had a hard time figuring things out. That's why it took so long for him to decide to leave the physical world. He talks about food. He could smell food but couldn't eat it! He's showing me more confusion over that. He says, 'I can't believe I'm about to say this'—Missy stops and laughs—*I would have thought this was bullshit too. He says you are the calm in the storm. He knows you held his hand and told him it was okay before he passed. He says he was afraid for half a minute and then left. He knows this is all part of your journey. You will be in service to others over what has happened in your life. You were angry over the events. He knows it sucks, but the events are here to serve you. You are getting so much out of this. It is part of your* **soul contract.** *I know this is funny coming from me. I was not this type. Love and life never*

die, time is nothing. He says lots of gratitude. He mentions dogs, and he shows me birds."

I explained that he raised hunting dogs, and they hunted pheasant and quail. Missy said, *"Yes, birds are a sign for you."*

Missy told me that my mom was chomping at the bit.

"Dad is needing care. He may not see it, but he is very stubborn and doesn't let you know things. Nothing imminent at this point, but his memory is failing. Father is worried about it and is aggravated about it. He's not saying, but is worried. It is not Alzheimer's, but he is afraid of that. Mom says she wasn't a good patient and was difficult to deal with. There's tubes, she does not like them."

Missy asked, "Is your younger sister a pain in the ass? *Is she a martyr? Do you take good care of her?*

At that point Missy started to fidget and explained that the information was scattered and not making sense.

I said, "Yeah that would be correct. That's how it always was with my mom—scattered, incomplete information."

I further explained that most times my mom would dance around the subject. There was seldom a direct focus, which led to a lot of guessing on my part. With that Missy held up her notepad she had been writing on and showed me the word *DANCE*.

"I was going to ask if you liked to dance or took dance as a kid or something, but that explained why dance came through." Missy laughed.

My mom continued, *"Regardless of how difficult I was, you still took good care of me."*

Missy said, *"Your mom is coming in as hateful, and I get a bitter, angry feeling. Letting you know she can turn it on and off. She can act totally fine but not be fine. In her daily life, she was overwhelmed. Overwhelmed with kids in the house. Housework, that was why she had the attitude, she couldn't handle it. She's hypersensitive, sounds, tastes and smells triggered a response. She's annoyed, everything was annoying. She doesn't give you the love you need. She is not very affectionate, not emotional, she's just not that person. Psychosis, mental illness, self-medication comes in the form of not being present. She was depressed and secluded herself.*

Missy adds, *"This is so much of your journey."*

Missy looked up and said, "You must be very spiritual, coming into that. Your messages are so big. You chose this, and she is part of it. She loves you."

Missy continued channeling my mother. "*You are beautiful. Absolute apologies are coming through. She acknowledges that she wasn't who you needed her to be, truly part of your journey. In your dreams or your meditations, things are happening that are important. They are real, seen, and heard . . . all real! Mom has already said apologies, she is not mushy: she messed up in life. She's not right, she wants you to know that your sister is not right either. It's okay that you've set boundaries for yourself. Don't feel guilty. She knows it doesn't mean that you don't love or care about them. You are in a place that you need to care about yourself. This is very healthy and very good. It doesn't have to be all or nothing. You are stronger. It gets easier, accepting your sister with her flaws. You shouldn't take it personally. Boundaries. Ask a lot of what ifs. Nothing is set in stone, not forever. Pay attention to your thoughts and focus. You are increasingly becoming more aware. Stay on your path. Your health concerns are fear-based because you've seen a lot of crap. Be more mindful. Focus on wellness for wellness's sake, not because you are afraid. Be mindful of your wellness journey."*

Missy confided after the reading that most of her readings are messages from dead people. But mine were more about dead people working with her, through me. Missy was so generous with her time, and I was so grateful to be the recipient of her special gift.

Receiving my mom's apology was one of the single most important messages for me. The amount of love and support that came through was profound. I felt the energy in the room. There was so much information available for me. I had an enormous amount of gratitude for the reading, the messages, and for Missy.

I was able to surrender in a whole new way after my reading. I received validation and heard what I needed. It was yet another tool to allow me to trust in my own intuitive wisdom. I felt spiritually healthier and wiser. There was more work to be done. There will always be more work, but I felt I had been given a precious gift. I felt recharged with an added benefit of having the support of spirit.

Teaching Moment: Following my intuition proved to be quite helpful for me and my healing journey. Yes, I have always had a curiosity about mediumship. Perhaps more than a curiosity, perhaps more like a genuine interest in how mediums work. At my core, I've always been open-minded. I say "at my core" because I believe the inquisitive side of unconventional subjects were off the table of comfortable discussion for me. Wouldn't want anyone to judge what interested me. Wouldn't want anyone to think I was weird.

Whether it was age or wisdom or just plain not feeling comfortable in my own skin that drew me toward all the things that fascinated me (or a combination of all of it), I am here. Here to experience and embrace this magical, wonderful, hard, and mysterious life.

Train your head to think like your heart. When they are working in tandem, nothing is too far out of reach. My dad always told me to think positively, but I know that it goes deeper than that. I know, in order for things to appear on my path, I have to believe positively. As long as my mind, body, spirit, and heart are in coherence, anything is possible. I know that if I stay in a state of gratitude, I will attract abundance in my life.

Follow your heart and stay true to who you are. Be patient and all things will happen in divine timing.

Chapter 36

Blades of Grass

We are but seeds, planted anew, sprouting up weak and vulnerable. This is understood and while some are very careful not to step on or damage the new seedlings, tiny, bright, and emerald green, others appear careless. Everything in the environment is enormous and unknown, but the inexperienced are fearless to explore with no comprehension of judgement or ego. A small blade of grass looks to the sky for the sun to nurture it, water to feed it, and air to test it. At some point when it is thought the blade of grass is becoming increasingly sturdier, some no longer walk around it but step on top of it. Some glance beyond it, never noticing how strong it has become . . . Some will yank it from the roots and discard it carelessly, while still others will intentionally pull it from the earth and allow it to plant itself elsewhere.

I sat in silence contemplating the symbolism of nature and more specifically the earth beneath me with its expansive, lush covering. I watched as the long blades swayed in the wind. How, as a group methodically in unison, they flowed in kinship. I had been experiencing some struggles lately that I was unable to put my finger on. I described it to a friend as *a lot of chaos, like blades of grass that are standing straight up but moving in all different directions.* That comment was paying a visit this morning. I thought about how symbolic so many parts of nature are to me. If I pay attention, all of the answers are there, deep within *my* nature. Like grass, we are connected to this earth, our mother, our nurturer. Our roots grow deep beneath her surface, anchoring our foundation securely connected to everything and everyone.

In meditation this morning, I tried to breathe the light in through my crown, but it would only enter through my third eye. Then I took the hand of my inner child and invited her to join me.

She said, "Thank you, it's about time."

And I said, "But I always think of you and include you in my every day."

And she said, "Yes, but you always hold me. This time I am walking with you, beside you. I like it here."

My meditation took me to my childhood hurts, and by that I mean physical injuries. A broken nose at the age of five. Standing a little too close to a friend, swinging her wooden baseball bat. A minibike accident that left me scraped up and bruised. I went into shock while my mother bandaged me up. My countless sprained fingers and sprained ankles. I saw my mom there to hold me and patch me up. I then recalled the emotional pain of loss: my pets, my grandparents, my in-laws, and my mom. In my third eye, I saw a violet light. I watched it as it swirled around like a lava lamp. It turned to amber brown, and then it turned into a cat's eye. It returned to a violet lava lamp and back to the cat's eye. After I arrived back into my physical body, I researched the symbolism of a cat's eye, and I found that cats can represent intuition and the subconscious. The magic in their eyes encouraged a belief that cats were seers with strong powers. The eyes of a cat are perhaps the most vital of a cat's features. Their pupils can dilate to a half inch in width and as narrow as a tiny slit. Cat's eyes represent mediumship.

My meditations have been getting more interesting and revealing. I also read, "Man And His Symbols," by Carl G. Jung about signs and symbols. It was an intensive read, but I got through it, and it proved to be very interesting for me. It taught me that the feelings and inner knowing that I connect with have been around for centuries, in all cultures, religions, and regions. Signs can be communication from the Universe, from Source, from your spirit guides, and from your angels. Many clues are sent to communicate in ways unexpected. They—spirit or other higher-realm communicators—are very creative, to keep our interest and to keep us thinking.

In this morning's meditation, my third eye was activated. My meditations play like movies, keeping me curious, and I've learned to surrender and allow my meditation to take me wherever it is I need to go. I saw vivid colors. They were bright and bewitching and mimicked a lava lamp, the way it had the other day. It was quite a show, and all of a sudden the color left and I could see something far off in the distance slowly coming into view. I couldn't make out what it was, and then as it came in closer, I could make out the shape. It was a symbol . . . followed by another symbol and yet another. The symbols passed right in front of me, in front of my third eye. I saw a star shape with no inside lines; I recognized it as the Merkaba star. (I had seen this before and previously researched it.) The next symbol I recognized but could not identify was a cross with a loop at the top and two lines that crossed through the center. Next was an hourglass, then a sphere. It was earth. Then a sphere with waves in it. Then I saw waves and water. I was flying in the air, weightless, like an astronaut in space. I was landing and pushing off and then floating. I was soaring through the air with angels. Then I landed and began walking, and I dove into a huge body of water. I was under the water, and marine life swam all around me. I was able to see everything that lived in the water, and they were swimming with me. As I swam alongside whales, dolphins, and fish, I felt the unjust human treatment of aquatic life. I was still in the water when I noticed there was land in front of me. It was a handsome, lush green. The greenest green I had ever seen. It was Ireland. *Why am I here?* I wondered. *Is it ancestral?* My meditation ended, and I was jolted back to my physical body.

That meditation experience was fantastic. *Why was I brought back so abruptly?* I wanted to share my amazing experience but didn't have anyone equipped to help me analyze it. *People are going to start thinking I'm making this shit up,* I thought. I decided that it would be a good time to pick up the deck of tarot cards I had purchased a while back. I looked through them briefly but hadn't learned how to work with them yet.

I shuffled the deck and flipped over the first four cards. I picked up the first card to study the face and connect with what I felt as I looked at it. I couldn't believe what I was seeing. The first card I flipped over had the symbols that I had just seen in my meditation. I had not noticed these on the tarot cards before. One could argue that I saw them and subconsciously memorized the images, but I didn't recall seeing any symbols from this tarot deck. The images on the cards were so intricate and busy that I felt more overwhelmed than anything. The synchronicity between my meditation and the symbols on the tarot cards was interesting to me.

The next day, I shared my meditation experience with Karen, and I tried to explain what some of the symbols were by describing what they looked like. She was able to identify the cross-like shape with a loop at the top. It is called an ankh loop and is known as the key of life. It was the ancient Egyptian hieroglyphic character that meant eternal life. Egyptian gods carried the ankh by the loop, or held one in each hand crossed over their breast.

I thought, *I can't wait to see what interesting images I will see next time I meditate.*

Teaching Moment: My meditations can either play like a movie or can feel sporadic and confusing, like a dream. I feel it is important to honor any feelings that come up while meditating. I believe we are to honor the imagery that is presented to us, and much like dreams, the imagery presented in meditations are to assist in guiding us to our truth. There is more for me to experience, and with each meditation I am learning more.

Be patient. Let go of your external attachments to people, places, and things, and breathe. My goal, at this point, is to get lost in the moment. I know more stillness brings more answers. I no longer feel as if I am doing it wrong. I never was. I needed to become comfortable with it. As soon as I did that and set an intention to surrender, my experience changed.

Chapter 37

See Me

Amy, my first yoga teacher, is so important to me. She is authentic, nurturing, and has a unique ability to challenge me. Her methodology invites me to perform to the best of my abilities. I have had the privilege of being on the receiving end of her knowledge of the human body. She has furthered her studies to include a more in-depth knowledge of muscles, tendons, bones, and fascia, which she incorporates into her yoga classes. I have also worked with Amy one-on-one, to help with a torn rotator cuff injury. She has a sweet and giving spirit. She has taught many informative workshops that introduced different facets of spirituality, including a chakra workshop and a meditation workshop.

I was thrilled to learn that our yoga class following my last meditation would be focused on our inner child. She asked us to look around the yoga studio and picture everyone at five years old. She asked us to be fearless, creative, and playful. I had been focusing on my inner child recently and making efforts to connect with the playful innocence of childhood, so the theme resonated with me.

I decided to be my five-year-old self during the entire sixty-minute practice, and I pictured all of the students as their five-year-old selves for the entire class. I found myself smiling *a lot*! I pictured myself as the girl in the Aunt Patty picture. It is my favorite picture of me and the one that I envision when I meditate and connect with my inner child.

During final *savasana*, Amy guided us in meditation. She encouraged us to walk in a field and to see our five-year-old self in the distance. She asked us to walk toward her and to picture the clothes she was wearing, to touch her hair, and caress her cheek.

"Pull her toward you, and give her a big hug," she instructed. "Tell her she is loved and cared for. Then let her run and play."

While embracing my inner child, I remembered doing something and getting my parents' attention by saying, "Look at me." The moment I got my parents' attention, I would become shy and all at once not want them to look at me. At that moment I had a breakthrough. All this time, I had labeled the desire to have my parents look at me or ask them to notice me, to be negative, like an egocentric adult attention-getter. In that moment, however, I realized it was the innocent, childlike, creative, playful me saying, "Look at me," out of love, not fear. Out of confidence, not judgment. Out of playfulness, not shame. It was an amazing acknowledgment. At the end of the meditation, I lay crying, feeling such a profound connection to my inner child, thanking her for delivering an accurate answer for me. To realize that I had held on to so much shame about drawing attention to myself was a lightbulb moment for me. I rolled up my mat and thanked Amy for a beautiful practice. She came over and hugged me.

She formed the words, "I love you."

She must have witnessed my moment, and that made me cry even more as I tried to form the words, "I love you too."

I could see the girls on either side of me, looking, as if to say, *did we miss something?*

All I could think was, *Gosh, I hope not!*

***

I started getting more visits from my deceased loved ones. The visits would occur during the end of my yoga practices.

They would begin with a simple knowing that they were with me. Then I would begin to feel their energy. Then I would actually see them. At first, like when I saw my mom in Ashley's yoga class, her image was very close to my face. Then I began to see their entire form as they stand in front of me. There would always be a message that accompanied their visit. The message was a simple knowing. Their mouths never moved, but I would hear the message and be aware of who was delivering the message.

The following evening, at the close of Ashley's class, Neno, my grandma on my mom's side, came in. I was in the final pose, and I saw her standing just off to my left. Her mouth was not moving, but she was speaking to me. She was there to deliver a message.

She said *"Thank you. Thank you for breaking the pattern. You were the only one with the nads to do it. You did the right thing, you made all the right choices."*

I could hardly believe my ears. It was exactly how Neno would have talked. She was a straight shooter and didn't mince words. She looked as she always had to me. She was very petite in stature but standing with intention. As Neno delivered her message, I saw a woman start to come out of the darkness several feet behind my grandma. The woman poked her head around sheepishly and looked like she was about to say something. Just then my grandma caught a glimpse of her, turned to the side, and shouted in a very stern voice, "*Hey!*"

My grandma was perturbed and annoyed that this woman had interrupted our talk. The woman faded back into the darkness, but just then I got a name . . . *Barbara.*

My grandma left and I lay on my yoga mat dumbfounded. *What the hell was that?* I wondered. I had a strong sense that someone in the yoga studio knew someone named Barbara. I wondered if it could be a dead relative of anyone gathered there.

It was the strangest thing I had encountered in a long time. I felt an urgency to figure out who Barbara was. We were asked to come to a seated position. I thought, *I'll ask some of the students before I leave, and find out.* I sat there a while longer, picturing the conversations that would ensue. *What if someone told me that yes, they did have a dead relative named Barbara? What then? What the hell would I say after that? That I just saw her? Then what?* I decided to stay quiet and keep it to myself. Feeling energetically like

I had been hit by a freight train, I gathered my belongings, quietly said my goodbyes, and left. While driving home, I couldn't stop thinking about it and wondered what I should do about it. *What does it mean? It's pretty damn cool, but what the hell?*

Experiencing visits from my dead relatives felt profound and powerful. It was one of the most real and genuine experiences, but I had no idea how I was going to share it with anyone. There was a part of me, however, that questioned it. *Perhaps I just have an overactive imagination*, I thought. If I were to share these experiences, I could just imagine the reactions I would get. Perhaps people would say, Come back to reality! Come back to the real world! *What if this is my real world?* I thought. I went back and forth, trying to figure out what I was supposed to do with the visit from Barbara. *Why did it happen?* I asked myself. *It was so strange. Is my grandmother trying to tell me something? Was Barbara trying to get my attention to let someone else know she was there? Even if she was, who am I to divvy out those details?* So many questions. So many feelings *Real. Not real.* But I *knew* it was real. I didn't manifest Barbara; she appeared. I couldn't have even *fantasized* about something like that happening.

After lengthy deliberation, I decided to share my experience with Ashley, my yoga teacher and friend. At our next class, I waited until there were just a few people around, and I said, "Can I ask you something?"

"Of course," she said.

"Have you ever experienced or heard of anyone experiencing intuitive-type things during their yoga practice?"

"No, not me personally."

She was intrigued, and I continued to explain what had happened in her class the other evening. She told me that she thought it was an amazing experience and was genuinely interested and offered her support. She made what felt like a vulnerable experience okay to share, and I was so grateful to have Ashley in my life. She had never heard of anyone experiencing anything similar during their yoga practice, so I decided that I should talk to Missy, the medium, and ask her for guidance.

I found an email address and I wrote to Missy, outlining my experience in detail, and I asked for her guidance and expertise. Missy responded, and the timing proved to be perfect. A couple weeks prior, she had started a tarot card reading class, and she invited me to be a participant. She explained that tarot was how, as a young girl, she learned about and strengthened her intuitive gifts. I was excited, confused, and a bit shocked. Missy's response supported the idea that I had the ability to connect with the other side. This was exciting and a bit freaky. I was excited to learn more but not necessarily through tarot cards. I had never been good at baby steps or the bunny hill. When I jump in, I want to go full bore, balls to the wall, expert hill right off the bat. Admittedly, that was my impatience rearing its all too prominent head. I reminded myself to relax and slow down.

Before I attended my first class, Missy sent some class instructions so that I could start working with the tarot deck that I had bought several months ago, right away. With everything feeling in alignment, I talked to Russ about my experience with Neno and Barbara and also the conversation I had had with Missy. He was a little shocked as to what I experienced, just as I was, but he supported me in whatever I felt I should pursue.

I was nervous but excited for my first class. Missy gave an overview, and I believed I would learn what I needed to learn, with her guidance. Most of our work, while in class, included a broad overview of tarot, learning the names of the different types of cards and their basic meaning. It was up to us, however, as the interpreter, to pay close attention to our personal feelings over and above the written meanings of each card. During the last portion of the class, we were to do an actual reading for and with fellow students. This proved to be very nerve-racking for me. I had no idea I would be asked to deliver a reading at my first class, let alone for Missy! Missy was helpful and supportive, but I'm pretty sure my first reading sucked.

I was diligent and I did the homework that was offered so that I could learn what I needed to know about my intuitive gifts. I realized how my meditation practice had prepared me for the tarot work. In fact, I believed it was the art of getting quiet that allowed this to find me in the first place. As time went on, I began to feel more confident about my readings, as people confirmed that I was spot-on with the information I received and then shared. Practice and positive comments boosted my confidence exponentially.

At my third class, Missy told us about her spiritual gatekeepers and how they've helped her in her work as a medium. She explained that she trusts them and that her relationship with them has grown over time. Before we got started in selecting our gatekeepers, she presented some guidelines. Our gatekeepers would be whoever entered our space, and we would see them as they were to be seen, by us, individually. Missy invited our class to begin with a short meditation. We had done short meditations in our classes prior to our readings, and I had been able to feel the energy in the room change. In the gatekeeper meditation, I experienced a great deal of bright light, but I also experienced a great deal of pressure. A change that I would describe as a similar feeling of going up in an elevator very fast, in a very tall building.

After our brief meditation, Missy instructed us to connect with our spiritual gatekeepers. I was able to get into my quiet space during meditation quite easily, so when Missy instructed us to meet our gatekeepers, I was ready and felt very open and relaxed. I was greeted by a very strong presence. It was a woman, and I sensed that she had a *take-no-shit*-type of personality. There was some discussion between another woman who I did not know and my potential gatekeeper, as to her name. The first name that I heard was *Francesca.* The argument was about me not being able to remember that name. They decided that the name I would remember was Angelica. As soon as her name was decided, a broad smile appeared on my gatekeeper's face, and I could feel her full presence. I could see her entire form and what she looked like. Angelica was a very strong black woman with a large frame and a commanding presence. I was aware that she was not going to take any shit from anyone and she had no problem speaking her mind. She was in charge, but she also had a big heart filled with pure love.

The next person I adopted, or the one that adopted me, was Sven. Sven was a small, blond, gay man who was sensitive and sweet. I thought the two of them made a good team and offered a good balance. Missy also told us that we could set boundaries for our gatekeepers, so I decided to declare mine while our relationship was brand-new. I asked both Angelica and Sven to only allow into my spiritual world and my earthly world people who offered love, support, and kindness as well as something to teach me.

Teaching Moment: Seek out people who possess the skills to teach you or assist you in your endeavors. Instruction and support are important in any classroom, but the subject of talking to dead people narrows the field of support. I trusted my gut and divulged a secret to my dear friend Ashley. She was supportive, which allowed space for me to steer toward a different direction. I spoke with Missy and learned how to hone in and develop my intuitive skills. After receiving guidance and pursuing a plan of action, I told my husband. I am surprised at how receptive and supportive Russ is to my strange experiences. I continue to broaden my perspectives, my acceptance, and my knowledge. But sometimes I think, *I wonder when it will be too weird for Russ to support me.* With some professional training under my belt, I felt confident enough to begin tarot card readings with family and friends. I studied and practiced every day. If not with someone else, I pulled cards every day for myself. Reading tarot is about trusting your instincts and your intuition. It's about creating a psychic library of signs and symbols and attaching personal imagery and feelings to them. It's about being aware and paying attention. It's a perfect complement to my other practices.

MY SOUL CONTRACT

Chapter 38

Team Spirit

I was in final *savasana* in yoga and for the first time, I deliberately asked for spirit to visit. The first to arrive was my Uncle Dave, and he brought Neno and Papa. Papa was my focus, and I connected with him immediately. I recalled how I felt in his presence. Seeing him in front of me, I felt safe and protected, loved and comforted. I saw him with a cigarette hanging off his lip and working on his art. I felt as if a heavy blanket were being laid on top of me, followed by an undeniable feeling of total calm and bliss. I felt like, Papa is here. Spirit is captivating. I am feeling *his* losses and *his* heartaches. The loss of his wife, my grandma. The loss of his grandson. I am also feeling how he felt when his son came to join him and when my mom came to join him. I could physically feel how his heart ached; it was heavy, just like the blanket. I could feel the sadness he felt for us, the ones left behind. He was grateful that his loved ones were with him. I told him that I was sorry he had to feel this pain. Then I was transported to his garage, and I recalled how I felt when he would work and I would watch. He was a good man, and I was grateful he was my Papa. I miss him.

I invited my spirit guides and my gatekeepers to join me, and they all came running in and lined up like the von Trapps.

I assured my guides that this was just to sit with me, so please relax.

I sort of giggled to myself as I could tell Angelica was caught off guard, and Sven looked as though he had just woken up from a nap. They were very charismatic, these two. I had a quiet meditation, and then a memory came.

It was Christmas when my dad got laid off from work. My dad had received the news one week before Christmas. I remembered my mom telling the story about how rotten that felt, and when we were old enough to understand she told us that she had all of our gifts wrapped and stored in the attic. She had to get them down, unwrap them, and return them to the stores. The memory I was recalling was opening the *replacement gift*. I could smell the contents as I opened the lid. It was a large plastic tote filled with colored construction paper, stencils, markers, chalk, colored pencils, glitter, glue, scissors, tape, coloring books, and crayons. Anything and everything craft-related was in that box. I loved that gift. In fact, that was one of my favorite Christmases of all time as a child. It was simple and I felt loved and taken care of. "Simple" felt *really* good. I remembered we colored and cut and crafted all day.

Putting myself in my parent's shoes, I could imagine the anguish they must have felt, but for me it was the best ever. I thanked my guides for bringing back this memory and for reminding me of the love that was wrapped inside that Christmas.

As I continued to sit in meditation with my spirit guides, more childhood memories came flooding in. I was at my grandma's house chewing on coffee grounds and eating the small dog biscuits she used to feed her poodle. (Yes, I did these things.) Then I was transported to my house, and I was diving, belly first, over the bushes in the front yard. Performing daring stunts on my minibike and getting hurt doing both. I was seeing and feeling all of it. I was a tomboy. I enjoyed a dare, and if I was told to "go for it," I did, as if I had something to prove.

I sensed someone near me, and it felt familiar. Someone was pushing through a crowd of people who had gathered around. As he made his way to the front, I recognized him. It was Arlington, my husband's paternal grandfather. Both Arlington and Catherine, Russ's grandma and grandpa, came through. They thanked me for making the album. Years ago I had taken all of Catherine's albums and removed the pictures and used acid-free, lignin-free products to create a photo-safe album. I included all of her original hand-written journal entries to preserve all of the precious memories, and I presented it to Dad Abels as a Christmas gift. It was a lot of work. I learned so much about my husband's family, and it was a wonderful experience for me. I thanked her for her well-narrated stories, and I also thanked her for the butter cookie recipe. Russ and the boys looked forward to the butter cookies every Christmas. Catherine shared a tip: *Use more lard.* They left, and I thanked them for their visit, and I thanked my gatekeepers for their guidance.

Chapter 39

Past Lives

I began today's meditation asking for guidance, knowledge, and understanding. I was guided into the unknown, black Universe, with my inner child. We were floating, feeling the abundance of our life. The word "constituted" came to me. I was taking in the endless, vast universe as I was being transported to another time. I understood that I was about to be shown a past life of mine. My inner child and I were traveling to a place I had never been. I didn't recognize it, but it felt safe. My inner child felt safe and understood why we were on this journey.

I was standing in front of a teepee. The canvas that made the door was folded back to reveal an Indian in full headdress, tending to a patient inside. I understood *this is me*. I was being shown a past life as an American Indian, a medicine man to be exact. I was shown validation that all we need to heal ourselves is in the earth and within our bodies. This culture, so rich in knowledge, validated what is available to us. I just have to look for it. As I turned to leave the teepee and prepare to return to my physical body, I reached out and held a bright, luminous star. I pulled it toward my chest and placed it in my heart. I could feel it, and it was warm and alluring. I looked at my inner child and pulled her close to me. I held her tight, and the bright light of the star jumped into her heart and illuminated her chest. We held on to each other tightly as we descended and traveled back to the body.

That night I began dreaming. I was in a crowded room full of people I was supposed to know, yet no one looked familiar. I felt claustrophobic and frustrated, and I wanted to leave, but I needed to find someone. I called out a name, "Caduce, Caduce, Caduce." I woke up and looked out into my bedroom and said the name out loud. My eyes were open, but I felt as if I was still dreaming. I said the name once more and lay back down. I drifted back to my dream. I was back in the crowded room. I saw the man I was looking for. He was holding a staff, and I knew why I was there. I was searching for Hermes. I knew that Hermes represented a past life. I woke up.

I was certain my dream was validating the meaning behind some recent meditations and confirming my beliefs. I was intrigued to look up the names that were so prominent in my dream. Hermes is a Greek god who served as herald and messenger to the other gods, otherwise known as "conductor of the dead." He carried a winged staff entwined with two snakes, called the "Caduceus." Today the Caduceus is used as a medical symbol. My dream exposed me to another past life. My dream secured my conviction of healing through my spirituality. And for some crazy reason a Greek God, who was the conductor of the dead, was the one I was looking for so that I would understand the symbolism offered in the nighttime acknowledgment of the name Caduce.

Thoughts and visits and symbols come to me all the time now. As soon as I sit quietly, it starts. I feel as if I have opened the floodgates. I am aware and am interested in the visits I encounter. I revisit the recent series of events that have offered me support to safely navigate this path even further. I have many cheerleaders, family, friends, and loved ones—my tribe members who continue to support me and are genuinely interested in my new discoveries. I am reminded of a phrase, "Build it and they will come." It is exactly how I feel. My continued interest and awareness have invited a nonstop parade of infinite exposure to an endless field of answers.

It is intense, but I am loving every minute of this magic. Within the past month the visits and messages have become stronger and more meaningful.

Teaching Moment: In meditation, nothing needs to be spoken. There is silence and a simple understanding. I am shown certain things, and I know instinctively the reasons why I am traveling to these places, and their meaning. I understand the intended purpose of each message that is presented to me. I feel abundant love and support as each detail unfolds. My meditations illuminate my truths and unravel an inner knowing. When I arrive back to three-dimensional reality, I am in awe of what I have just experienced and learned. Not all my meditations are like this. Sometimes, when I am unable to detach from my physical environment, very little happens, and it is an exercise of physical stillness. But when I am able to leave everything that I'm attached to in my three-dimensional reality behind, I am awestruck time and time again as I experience each event and what is being offered to me.

MY SOUL CONTRACT

Chapter 40

Building My Psychic Library

I was standing in the lobby of my bank. While I was waiting, a woman approached me and shared her experience of losing her husband. I nodded sympathetically while she continued to tell me that her dead husband talks to her, and her son thinks she's crazy. I told her, "I know he talks to you, and you are not crazy, but you already knew that, and I believe you."

As I left the bank, I pondered the conversation and how differently I would have handled it years ago. It was nothing new for people to share their struggles and their personal business with me. It used to make me uncomfortable, and I used to joke and ask if I had a sign on my back that read, "Tell me your deep, personal stuff that I shouldn't know about you." Today sorted some of that out for me. I understand that it's energy. I felt that this woman told me her story because an energy was present that allowed her to feel safe enough to approach me and share.

My mind drifts in final *savasana*. I am reviewing the souls, the spirits of dead people that I have seen that have surprised me because they were not my relatives, friends, or acquaintances. First, there was *Barbara*, the woman who interrupted my grandma while she was bringing me a message.

Next was *Maggie*. That experience occurred while I was standing in the IT department at work. Out of the blue a woman said the name *Maggie*. I of course didn't ask anyone in IT if they knew Maggie. It would have been too weird for them.

The third time was in yoga. I heard the name *Tyler*. Tyler was an infant but soon turned into a three- or four-year-old. When I questioned the age, the number three came up, and it was circled. *Is this three for the third month? Or is it the age of the child?* I wondered. Next I saw a yellow sand bucket and shovel that he was playing with on the beach. Someone lost this little boy, but who? I am not sure what the small boy meant for me. I decided that Tyler represents the loss of a child, and the sand bucket and shovel represent childhood memories.

I continued working daily with my tarot cards. I studied the images and paid attention to the thoughts and words that came through and practiced trusting the information. Each time I sat down to give myself a reading, I took a few moments to call in my gatekeepers. They work with me and bring me the symbols and messages that assist me to connect with spirit and the person I am reading. I've added one more to the two previously adopted gatekeepers. Bob is a very mainstream, even-tempered, ho-hum kind of guy. Tarot cards in hand, I invited Bob, Angelica, and Sven to assist me in the reading. They ran in and lined up like the von Trapps, which has become the norm. When I shared this in class with Missy, everyone laughed; it was comical the way I saw them stumbling around and lining up like little soldiers.

Missy asked, "Is that behavior familiar to you, perhaps something relatable in your childhood?"

"I never thought of that, but yes, it represented my childhood."

I recalled a vivid memory that supported my feelings on the matter. Back when you could leave children in the car safely for long periods of time, my mother left my sisters and me in the car while she grocery shopped. One of us sat in the front seat and sounded the alarm when my mom was headed back to the car. The other two siblings stayed in the back seat and beat the tar out of each other.

We bit and scratched, pulled hair, and spit on each other, up until the sister in the front seat sounded the alarm. Hair snarly, arms bleeding, we straightened our clothes and sat prim and proper while my mother loaded groceries in the trunk. We lined up just like the von Trapps.

Outwardly, everything was neat and tidy, obedient and orderly. We were laughing and joking; everything was controlled in our perfect façade. Inside was total confusion and disorder for me. My gatekeepers were emotional representatives for me.

I was in meditation, and I sat with my fingers in lotus position, opening and closing. My thoughts drifted to a memory of a childhood experience of picking lilacs from a neighbor's tree and giving them to my mother. As a mother, it's a difficult position. You want to teach your child right from wrong. Although it is wrong to pick other people's flowers regardless of the intention, it's difficult not to praise a child for her kind and loving gesture. My mom told me it was wrong and I had to walk back to the neighbor's house and confess what I had done. Then I had to apologize for picking her flowers without permission. I remembered feeling so bad and a little scared as I was ready to confess. The neighbor was sweet and thanked me for letting her know what I had done. She appreciated the apology and told me that I could keep the flowers to give to my mom. I also recalled a separate incident involving flower picking. I went along the entire row of tulips at our next-door neighbor's house and picked just the tops off of each one. My mother was not happy, and neither was Mrs. Schmidt. I will add Mrs. Schmidt and lilacs and tulips to my psychic library to use as symbols for innocent childhood lessons.

Missy taught us to build a library, to make a connection with the people who were communicating with us, along with the images that appeared, so that we could use them to help with our readings. The name Brian popped in today. He was a high school classmate, but it was his brother Paul who I was supposed to connect with. Paul committed suicide in his first year of college. It's weird how I was brought to one person, but then it passed to another person who I am supposed to use in my library. I thought of others who had also committed suicide. There was a girl in high school, and I had a friend in grade school whose mother took her own life. I have a friend now who shared with me that her mother also took her own life. I thought of the young man down the street, our neighbor, who committed suicide. There were too many in that library.

Teaching Moment: I thought of all the times I put myself out there and made myself vulnerable. Times when I spoke my mind and shared my truth. I thought about my grandma showing up as my cheerleader and saying, *"Cuz you had the nads,"* reminding me of her powerful message. Many experiences that once felt difficult have moved me into a different energy and introduced me to a higher version of myself. In confrontations, I am able to feel empathy for the other person. While I do not intend to hurt anyone, I do need to tell them how I feel. It is imperative that I demonstrate my value and honor my truth. This is the work. The work that asks you to show up every day. The work that prompts you to value yourself. The work that is an investment in your health and well-being. A message that states even though it may feel difficult, it is important to set healthy boundaries for yourself. Honor your truth and explore your own healthy boundaries. Write your own self-care prescription for all the things that feel right in your gut and in your heart. A mindful, healthy, and positive outcome is assured with this plan of action.

Remind yourself as often as needed to follow your heart and allow your depth. Never be ashamed of exposing your true self.

Chapter 41

Respite

Water, the symbol of emotion, supportive ebb and flow of life. Dreaming and daydreaming mixed together in a recipe of calming peace. Vacation, a gift of no time. Time to let go of deadlines, demands, and schedules. Water invites childlike logic to recharge my emotional batteries. Water, vital for our survival, proposes power and freedom and playfulness.

Vacation brain changes perceptions and perspectives.

Vacation. Water. Time.

Which is real? Which is not real?

I am daydreaming about vacation and thinking about how water holds powerful symbolism for me. Water represents emotion. It makes up more than 65 percent of the human body and is vital for our survival. The more I learn about the four earth elements and their symbolism, I become more aware of why water has always been a magnet for me.

We will be enjoying an abundance of water soon, and the thought of recharging our personal batteries is just a few days away. Vacation, a time to let go of our demands, schedules, and deadlines, and embrace the freedom from the everyday monotonous to-do lists, proves to be a much-needed respite. It's time to engage in our childlike logic, where time doesn't exist. The only thoughts of time, for me, while on vacation are when it begins and when it ends. *Wouldn't it be wonderful to operate from that perspective every day?* A gift of time for me would be when time doesn't exist. Why not make time to experience *no time*? Ironically, not being aware of time is some of what meditation offers me. Meditation has become a daily vacation for my mind.

I made myself go to yoga, partly because it's Ashley's class and partly because I will miss an entire week of yoga while on vacation. The last thing I thought I would be able to do was decompress and let go. I had so many things to do before vacation, and my mind and my thoughts were on overload. My practice has turned into a skill, and after a few deep, calming breaths, I was able to quiet my anxious mind.

Final *savasana* came and Ashley offered a gentle head and face massage. Before she completed the preliminary relaxation exercise, I started seeing images. I saw a close-up of a face of an older man, unshaven and disheveled. I didn't recognize him at first, but as he backed away I realized it was Al, a person I hadn't thought about in years. I remembered his sense of humor and the friendship he and my dad shared. He smoked a lot and drank a lot of coffee. He struggled on and off with his addiction to alcohol. He stood in front of me for a bit, and I wasn't quite sure why he was visiting. The folks who visit get to the business of delivering a message for me. Al was just standing there. I had never had that happen before, so I felt prompted to speak first. I asked Al if he was there for me to use in my psychic library. He told me that I could do that but he was also visiting because he had a message for me. (Al was much shyer than I recalled.) He told me that years ago, my mom had given my dad an ultimatum. He told me that my mom didn't like his behavior and that he had to make a choice between his family and his behavior. I remembered my mom sharing a similar statement with me years earlier, although I was not clear about the behavior and I didn't ask.

Al said, "Your dad would do anything for you girls, so he kept the family intact."

I thanked Al for the information and also for his willingness to work with me. He said that he could represent struggles with addiction to use in my intuitive work. Al was a good guy, and I was glad he had come to visit.

My next visit from Spirit was from the Schultzes. The Schultzes were our next-door neighbors when I was very small. I have very fond memories of that house and the neighbors. Our house was a two-bedroom ranch and was in between the Schultz's and a park. Mr. Schultz was a sweet grandpa-type, and I remembered how I felt in his presence. I don't remember too much about Mrs. Schultz. In fact, I couldn't even recall her first name. When I grew up and worked as a teller at our hometown bank, Mr. Schultz would bring me homemade turtles for a Christmas treat. Mr. Schultz was emphatic when he delivered the goodies. He wouldn't drop them off with the girls I worked with; instead, he made sure he handed them to me. I worked at the bank for ten years, and I don't think he missed one delicious delivery at Christmas.

I was developing more confidence with spirit, so I asked if he was visiting to work with me and to be part of my spiritual library.

He responded, "Yes, whatever you feel or remember when you think of me will be a symbol for you in your readings."

I thanked the Schultzes for their visit. My library was getting more resources!

The next morning, while I was driving to work, I was thinking of my visit with the Schultzes, and it was bothering me that I couldn't remember Mrs. Schultz's first name. Just then I saw a dead rabbit in the road. It was pristine and looked as if it were taking a nap. Usually seeing dead animals in the road, or anywhere for that matter, is difficult for me to see, and I would make myself look away. Even though it made me sad, this rabbit wasn't hard to look at.

I said out loud, "Poor bunny."

And then I remembered Mrs. Shultz's first name. It was Bunny! Thank you, spirit!

I attended Amy's ninety-minute hot yoga class. It was hot and humid outside, and the studio was even hotter and more humid. About forty-five minutes into our flow, I was overcome with nausea and had to take a seat on my mat. The nauseous feeling was not going away, so I moved into child's pose. After a short reset, I felt better and was up on my feet, following along with the rest of the class. I completed one more asana and was right back to feeling nauseous again. I knew the best thing to do was to listen to my body and sit back down on my mat. I observed the other students moving through the flow with little to no trouble. I was struggling and they were not. That was a bit of a head game for me. My body was screaming at me to stay put, but my ego wanted to compare and told me to get my butt up. I listened to my body and remained seated on my mat. After a few more poses, Amy moved to the back of the studio and opened the doors.

She said, "Okay, I see you're all dropping like flies in here."

With the doors open, cooler air entered the room. I was much more comfortable and was able to get through the last few poses. Our seventy-five-minute flow was over, which led me into the ultimate thank-you-God final *savasana.* Amy rarely played music during class. She taught us to listen to the class and synchronize our breath in unison with the entire class. But I heard music, glorious music. I loved lying there, being moved by the music and my practice.

A deep cleansing breath and the visits began. First Papa, then Neno, my Uncle Dave, Mom, Mom Abels, Dad Abels, my other grandma and grandpa, Other Neno and Bomp, Aunt Marge, Uncle Ben, and even Kath and Bob (my father's aunt and uncle.) I was overwhelmed by the sheer number of spirits. I observed as each one entered the room, and watched as the space filled up with my dead people, my spirit family. I was moved first by the music and then by the ensemble gathered before me, but nothing could have prepared me for what happened next.

As the music in the yoga studio came to an end, I watched as each spirit gathered before me transformed into a symbolic black-and-blue butterfly and fluttered away. I was brought back to the rock at the lake, where I had first experienced their compelling dance. Contentment filled my heart as tears welled up and offered a release of intense emotional gratitude.

Teaching Moment: The symbolism and the acknowledgment of how I felt that day at Lake Norfork compared to my experience in Amy's yoga class stilled my heart in a way that evaded all description. Being a witness in my own spiritual journey and seeing each ascended spirit transform into beautiful butterflies to match those that I saw on the rock so long ago validated my own transformation. A transformation that felt like it had brought me full circle. A transformation that has offered unexpected, jaw-dropping synchronicities. I no longer question what is real and what is not real. I invite any and all experiences and honor the intimate relationship I have with the path leading me back to whole. Whole represents a culmination of living through all of my experiences. Whole is the trust I have in my internal compass. Whole represents a deeper, more introspective understanding of self. Whole equals bliss. I'm glad I listened, and I'm glad I paid attention to the nudges. Glad and grateful.

Chapter 42

The Gifts

Lynn, who had been so generous with her time and expertise, presented each of her participants with mala beads to conclude our group meditation class for the summer. She said I should wear the beads for forty days to form a connection to this ancient meditation tool. On the forty-first day, I sat in my backyard and began my meditation with an intention. My intention has also become my daily mantra: *breathe, trust, and surrender*. During my meditation I had a connection with Mom and Dad Abels, and the visit was audibly interrupted by a name: Ezekiel. I continued with my meditation, but the interruption happened three or four more times. Although I didn't see a face or a person, I kept hearing the name Ezekiel. This intrigued me, so when my meditation was over I was anxious to do some research.

I learned that Ezekiel is the archangel of transformation. He adjusts the energy of those going through an experience of awakening and is there to help. I may experience symbols of sacred geometry. Merkaba in old Egyptian translation refers to a rotating light that takes the spirit and the body from one world to another. Merkaba, is the vehicle in which Ezekiel ascended to heaven.

The pieces of my spiritual puzzle were coming together. I had been seeing the symbols of sacred geometry in my early meditation practice. Sacred geometry is an ancient science that explains the energy patterns that create and unify all things. My sacred geometry experience began when I saw the ankh and the star-shaped symbol referred to as the Merkaba.

The Ezekiel meditation validated the importance of signs and symbols and further ignited my curiosity into the world beyond the physical. Something or someone was continuing to guide my attention, and I chose to trust the importance of the lessons in the messages.

During my next meditation, I was brought to a place I had been before. I was standing in front of me—me in a past life—the medicine man, the healer. I had met the Indian medicine man in a previous meditation and he was coming to help. He, as me, began to send energy through my entire body. He stood silent and communicated through thought alone. *You're healed and healthy. The pain you are experiencing in your neck can be remedied.* He started to move his hands around the silhouette of my body, and I felt a warm sensation passing through the palms of his hands. He placed his colossal hands tenderly around my neck and tilted my head slightly to the left. He pulled from the right side of my neck a long, rigid rod. The rod was equal to the entire length of my body. When the entire length was free from my body, he displayed it in front of me while saying, *"This is anger."* He laid it down horizontally on a ledge that was suspended in air behind him. He turned toward me and performed the same ritual on the left side of my neck. He held the rod in front of me and said, *"This is jealousy, lack, not good enough."* He carried it and placed it next to anger. He made a few movements with his arms in a ceremonial fashion and said, *"They are being sent to the fire, they are transforming, no more pain, no more lack and no more anger. They were no longer useful to you. They are gone. They are now your wisdom."*

He warmed his hands over the bright flame created by my rods of anger and lack. He cupped his hands over my left knee. The warmth transferred deep into the tissue and muscle. He was near my knee but not touching it. I felt the depth of healing that took place. He returned to the fire and held his hands over the flame and repeated the healing ritual on my right knee.

What I inherently understood to be *the transfer* was over, and he placed his hand on top of my head. I moved closer in front of him, and he pressed our bodies together. *We were heart to heart.* I felt the intensity of the energy from his heart moving into and entering my heart. He looked into my eyes while the transfer occurred, and I was so overcome with warmth that I thought I would pass out. He continued to look into my eyes when the transfer finished. There were no words, but I was aware that I must not waiver. I knew he was a great master.

I had never felt warmth at that level before. It was a deep warmth I felt throughout my body, my mind, and my spirit. I was to understand that the warmth symbolized unconditional love. The healer looked past my eyes deep into my soul and nodded his head as if he were pleased with the transfer. He turned and disappeared.

With an abundance of gratitude and joy, I was to return to my physical form with an elevated state of bliss and pure love. I was to return changed.

Teaching Moment: I am a changed person after meditation. When a mystical experience occurs in meditation, there is no other way to be than changed. How can you come back as the same person after experiencing such a transformative, life-changing event? You can't and who would want to? There is a lot of science that goes into explaining a perfect cocktail for a mystical experience, and my hope is that you get to experience at least one in your lifetime. First, be open-minded and enter into a dreamlike state. Dreams occur while our brain enters the theta brain wave frequency. Theta is the intriguing border between the conscious mind and the subconscious mind. While in theta, the mind is capable of deep and profound learning, healing, and growth. Second, while connecting to a higher consciousness, you are able to let go of your attachments to your physical body (telling you your legs hurt and your back hurts, begging you to stop the nagging discomfort of sitting still). You are also able to let go of your responsibilities and your to-do lists. Third, tap into your desires and begin to design your future. Fourth, set an intention. Pair your intention with the feelings of love, gratitude, or joy, and release that energy into the field. The field holds all potential. You will attract back to you what you put into the field. You must believe it to receive it. Fifth, be patient, and it will find you.

Trust. Breathe. Surrender.

Chapter 43

Rose

A flash. An enticing image. A sensory tease.

I observe.

A blonde-haired, pony-tailed girl dressed in a white, Peter Pan-collared yellow dress stands in white-laced anklets under a pair of shiny, white, patent leather shoes, and draws on the chalkboard with her friend. She turns the chalk sideways to create broad strokes. The chalk moves in a circular pattern, creating numerous dashes. She tries to mimic her grandfather. Her dark-haired friend tries to mimic her. The two eight-year-olds stand back to look at their artistic creations. They smile, feeling accomplished.

They smile, feeling they've created something admirable.

We are all intuitive and we all have gifts. Intuition is a gift we are born with. But over time, as outside influences and interests take over our busy lives, our intuition drifts away as we no longer trust or pay attention to it. Embracing the gifts of my intuition and acknowledging the signs and symbols that were presented to me on a daily basis were powerful resources to invite back into my life. The ability to quiet my mind and bring stillness to my body allowed me to embrace the gifts that presented themselves to me.

I was able to notice the synchronicities of my life's events. I wanted to learn more and open my heart to the places I had not yet explored. In the past few weeks I had been learning more about the symbolism of animals, specifically totem or spirit animals. A spirit animal is a teacher or a messenger that comes in the form of an animal and has a personal relationship with an individual.

It was early December 2017, and I was enjoying yoga at Julia's new studio. I met Julia at the yoga studio near work, and unbeknownst to me, we lived in the same town. I was thrilled to learn that she would be teaching at her new yoga studio so close to home. I felt the same way about Julia as I did about Amy and Ashley. They have different teaching styles, but their gentle, authentic, nurturing character made them my favorites.

I was at the end of my yoga practice, lying in the final resting pose when I received a gift. I experienced a flash, a quick image, a *sensory tease* in my third eye, my sixth energy center. It made me curious, and I tried to entice it back into view. I asked for it to return.

I wanted another opportunity to figure out what the image was. The feeling I had the moment the image came into my consciousness was the image of a child's familiar drawing. In fact, it was one of my own drawings from when I was a young girl. I used to draw flowers—roses to be exact. One of my drawing methods at that young age was to draw dashes. The dashes started in the center, and I worked my way out into a circular pattern. That was my interpretation and illustration of a rose, as if you were looking straight down at it. In a flash, I had a memory of my artwork as a child and in an instant, just a little glimpse of its imagery.

I didn't see the image again until the following week. I had forgotten all about it, and suddenly there it was again. During final *savasana*, the same image appeared, only this time it stayed a bit longer and it appeared a bit larger. It validated what I had thought originally. It reminded me of my childhood drawings of a rose. In repetition, each consecutive evening, I started seeing the image at the end of every yoga practice. With each visual, I was able to hang on to the image for a little longer. Each time it appeared, I felt there was something more for me to see and feel. A smile crossed my lips, and I felt such peace and calm in that moment.

During Thursday night's final *savasana*, I intentionally thought of the image. I invited it back, and as soon as my eyes closed, it was there again, my rose. The image was larger than it had ever been, and the magnification startled me. It was closer than it had ever been to me, and suddenly, without warning, the center opened up.

What an astonishing surprise. It was a gorgeous, dark amber-colored iris with long, magnificent, ebony eyelashes. As I realized what the image was, it was as if a camera were backing up to show me the full expanse of it. As soon as the lid opened, I knew it was an elephant's eye. As the camera zoomed out, the wrinkles around the elephant's eye were the dashes in my flower drawing.

I knew that I was experiencing an unfolding. I also knew I was not supposed to understand it the first time it appeared. I knew instinctively it held a deeper meaning. As I lay in quiet stillness, I watched as my mind movie played. The image showed itself, almost teasingly. It revealed its identity with such vividness, as if I could bring my hand to my third eye and actually touch and feel the magnificent creature. I was in awe, grateful for its presence. I wanted to open my eyes and see it standing in front of me, all the while knowing, as soon as I did, it would be gone. I was compelled to have a dialogue with the gorgeous giant.

I thanked the elephant for coming to me. Then I asked, "What is your name?"

"Rose."

She continued, "I am your spirit animal, and I am here for guidance."

A feeling of complete love and support washed over me, and tears of gratitude began to fall.

Yoga ended, and Rose was gone.

The next night, as soon as I closed my eyes to feel the benefits of my yoga practice, Rose appeared. I was standing right in front of her, gazing into her majestic eyes. I could feel all the minute hairs, the rough texture, and the soft, sensitive, agile tip as I ran my fingers down her trunk. She brought the end of her trunk up to my face and then lowered her trunk to the ground. She curled the end of her trunk to make a seat for me. As I lowered myself to sit in her swing, she swayed it side to side, gently rocking me. It was at that moment I knew I was to trust her. Rose told me she would be with me always, to love, support, and guide me. I could ask anything and she would be right next to me, and the answers would feel like instinct.

Rose is part of my spiritual entourage. When I call upon my gatekeepers, my spirit guides, and my angels, I will include Rose as one of my spiritual messengers.

The symbolism of the elephant is profound. Elephant, the ever gentle and wise spirit animal, represents focused power and strength. When an elephant appears in your life, it represents a new and improved relationship with the Sacred Feminine. Lightworkers tell us that elephant guides us toward a deeper understanding of the Mother or Crone to connect with our own positive feminine attributes. Elephants represent an intense focus on family, including past and future generations. Elephants also know that not all families are bound by blood. Sometimes people come into our lives that hold that sacred role energetically.

It is so good to be here, right here, right now, in this very powerful and generous present moment. I can gaze up with my arms spread wide open toward the sky and give thanks for every experience and every event. Whether the experience was negative, positive, or indifferent, I chose to pay attention and acknowledge that all were gifts presented to me in divine timing.

For the past fifty-five years there have been a great deal of changes in me. The first forty were a dress rehearsal for the life I thought I was going to live. But miraculously, the last fifteen have proven to be the life I was meant to live. I spent my first four decades believing I was fine until an event shattered my world and pulled the formidable rug out from under me. It forced me to reevaluate everything in my life. I didn't realize how shattered I was until I lifted the rug to see what was underneath. Beneath my shattered foundation were all the shattered pieces. The pieces I had been taught to sweep under, never to be looked at or talked about or felt or held.

I have the utmost gratitude for my mom and dad; without them, I would not have gone searching for my own answers. I am grateful for the upheaval and the shattering of my heart. I would not have known what was waiting for me on the other side of my crumbled foundation. I had depended not only on my parents my entire life but also my husband, family, and friends to hand me the answers. As I've learned, they never had the answers I needed. All my answers were intrinsically within me all along, buried with years of well-intentioned and some not so well-intentioned outside influences.

I needed my foundation to crumble. It forced me to build my own structure. A solid structure to the core built on my beliefs, my values, and my inner knowing. I hold love and gratitude for anyone who has traveled alongside me on this journey. I am grateful for all of my teachers and vow to remain curious and keep walking and learning and honoring my soul contract.

I invite you to do the same.

The End

Acknowledgments

Thank you to all my teachers. Thank you Mom and Dad, without you, I may have never found my true purpose and passion. Thank you Russ for the countless sacrifices while I typed away at my keyboard, organizing, and revising over, and over, and over again. Thank you for your continued support and your undying love. You are my rock, my center, and my forever love. Thank you Nick and Derrick. Because of you, my favorite name is "Mom." You are my fuel. You will forever be my greatest teachers. Thank you for your unwavering support, your love, and your genuine interest while I pursued this writing endeavor. You are amazing men and I am beyond proud to call you my sons. Thank you Heidi for your unwavering support. You are an astounding woman, a true, blue friend and my forever cheerleader. Thank you for being a "pen" friend. Thank you for every conversation and every glass of wine shared. Thank you Amy, Ashley and Julia, without your passion, I would not have fallen in love with the practice of yoga. Thank you Karen for being my first spiritual teacher, having a kind heart and providing a safe place to share my experiences. Thank you Missy for teaching me about your intuitive gifts and providing your guidance so I could embrace mine. Thank you Kel, for being my big sis, my sounding board and a much-needed support while our family fell apart. Thank you to all my beta readers and pre-published book club reviewers for your time and your heartfelt feedback, Susan B., Susan P., Heidi, Ashley, Christa, Eugenia, Gloria, Perla, Jenna, Colleen, Christine, and Jennifer. Thank you Ritta M. Basu, my developmental editor, for your honest feedback, patience, guidance and professional advice. Thank you Valerie Brooks, my copyeditor, for your expertise, insight, and guidance. Thank you Janine for your valuable time, expertise and feedback. I gained a new perspective that helped put the finishing touches in place and helped me "kill the little darlings." You all have made me a better writer and I owe you a debt of gratitude. Thank you Christine for your artistry, design and your attention to detail in creating the book cover. You make it look so simple. You were able to channel my vision and produce a perfect image based on the illustration that only lived in my head. Thank you to my dearly departed for your visits, support and guidance. Thank you to my gate keepers, angels, archangels and divine entities.

Thank you all for being a part of My Soul Contract.

Immense gratitude for each and every one of you